The Real World

Timeless Ideas
Not Learned in School

2nd edition

DAVID KRAMER

ROWMAN & LITTLEFIELD
Lanham • Boulder • New York • London

Published by Rowman & Littlefield
An imprint of The Rowman & Littlefield Publishing Group, Inc.
4501 Forbes Boulevard, Suite 200, Lanham, Maryland 20706
www.rowman.com

6 Tinworth Street, London SE11 5AL, United Kingdom

British Library Cataloguing in Publication Information Available

Library of Congress Cataloging-in-Publication Data

ISBN 9781475856026 (cloth : alk. paper)
ISBN 9781475856040 (electronic)

∞™ The paper used in this publication meets the minimum requirements of
American National Standard for Information Sciences—Permanence of Paper
for Printed Library Materials, ANSI/NISO Z39.48-1992.

To my parents, Harold and Lucy Kramer
To my great climbing buddy, Dave Vidrik

Contents

Foreword to the First Edition   xv

Foreword to the Second Edition   xvii

Acknowledgments   xix

Introduction   1
    We All Start Out the Same   1
    Credit for the Ideas in This Book   3
    How This Book Evolved   3

1 Entering the Real World   5
    1-1. Welcome!   5
    1-2. How You Will Benefit   6
    1-3. How to Use This Book   7

2 If You Are Still in School   11
    2-1. Looking for a Career?   12
    2-2. Use Your School's Career and Internship Services   13
    2-3. Start Preparing Now for the Real World   13
    2-4. Set Salary Expectations   18
    2-5. Introverts and Extroverts   19
    2-6. Boost Your Vocabulary and Writing Skills   19
    2-7. Avoid Negative or Questionable Digital Tattoos   20
    2-8. The Lost Art of True Browsing   20

2-9.   Learn from What You Have Already Accomplished   21
2-10. Common Mistakes While Still in School   21
       Takeaway Summary   22

3 Think for Yourself   23
3-1.   A Joy of Adulthood: Thinking for Yourself   24
3-2.   Don't Categorize People; Everyone Has a Story   24
3-3.   Choice and Opportunity in America   25
3-4.   Gratitude   26
3-5.   It's True! A Positive Attitude Helps!   27
3-6.   Live *Your* Life, Not Someone Else's   27
3-7.   Find Mentors of All Ages   28
3-8.   Intellectual Honesty   29
3-9.   "I Don't Know" and "I Made a Mistake"   29
3-10. Examples to Challenge Your Thinking for Yourself   30
3-11. Follow the Money   32
3-12. Be Careful with False Alternatives   32
3-13. Be Careful with Statistics   33
3-14. Failure as a Learning Tool   33
3-15. Two Poems for Tough Times   34
3-16. Common Mistakes While Learning to Think for Yourself   35
       Takeaway Summary   35

4 Communicating with Others and Yourself   37
4-1.   Get Your Point Across in Thirty Seconds or Less   38
4-2.   What Do You Mean? Define Your Terms   38
4-3.   How Do You Know You Are Right?   41
4-4.   All Facts Are Opinions; Not All Opinions Are Facts   42
4-5.   When Are the Masses Right?   43
4-6.   "Whose Problem Is It?"   44
4-7.   Abraham Lincoln and the Cow's Tail   45
4-8.   Who Has the Risk in an Outcome?   45
4-9.   Should You Write, Call, Meet, E-mail, Text, Send a Video?   46
4-10. Relationships   47
4-11. Conflict Resolution   48
4-12. Public Speaking in Front of Two or Two Hundred People   49
4-13   What Are Your News Sources and Why?   50

4-14. Advertising's Impact on Your Life   50
4-15. Look People in the Eye   51
4-16. No "Digital Tattoos"   51
4-17. Clean Up Your Social Media   51
4-18. Common Mistakes in Communication   51
       Takeaway Summary   52

5 Entering and Adjusting to the Workplace   55
5-1.   Interviewing   56
5-2.   Getting Great Reference Letters   61
5-3.   Sidebar: When Asking for Favors   62
5-4.   Getting Great Raises   62
5-5.   Negotiating for the Win-Win   63
5-6.   Protect Your Most Valuable Asset in the Real World   65
5-7.   Define Your Ideal Company   65
5-8.   How to Get Ahead at Work   67
5-9.   How to Prepare Impressive Reports and Presentations   68
5-10. Lose the Excuses!   69
5-11. Advance One Job or Position at a Time   70
5-12. People Skills vs. Technical Skills: Which Is Harder to Develop? 70
5-13. Accountability   71
5-14. Responsibility and Authority   72
5-15. The 80–20 Rule   72
5-16. Legal Matters   72
5-17. Volunteering   72
5-18. Common Mistakes When Entering and Adjusting
       to the Workplace   73
       Takeaway Summary   73

6 Life's Situations with Challenging Personalities   75
6-1.   Working Alongside Different Personalities   76
6-2.   Meeting a Gruff and Generally Unpleasant Person   76
6-3.   Meeting an Unhappy, Complaining Coworker   77
6-4.   Meeting Someone Who Wants to Steal Software or
       Other Company Assets   77
6-5.   Meeting Someone Who Follows a Different Religion   78
6-6.   Meeting Someone with a Mental Illness   78

6-7.	What Indicates a Mental Illness?	79
6-8.	Meeting Many Other Personalities	80
6-9.	If Someone Close to You Dies or Leaves	80
6-10.	Look for a Win-Win	81
6-11.	Common Mistakes in Life's Situations with Challenging Personalities	81
	Takeaway Summary	82
7	**Personal Improvement**	**83**
7-1.	A Perspective on Personal Improvement	84
7-2.	Building Self-Esteem	85
7-3.	What Is Your Emotional Intelligence?	86
7-4.	Positive Self-Talk; or, What Do You Think of Yourself?	86
7-5.	Your Mindset	87
7-6.	Determining Your Strengths and Weaknesses	88
7-7.	Goal Setting	89
7-8.	"The Stress of Life"	90
7-9.	"Getting Things Done"	90
7-10.	Use a To-Do List	91
7-11.	"Good" and "Bad" Judgment	93
7-12.	Set Personal Boundaries and Expectations	94
7-13.	Dignity, Honor, and Respect	94
7-14.	Impossible vs. Possible vs. Hard	95
7-15.	Would You Guarantee Your Work?	95
7-16.	Yet There Are No Guarantees in Life	96
7-17.	Ignorance and Awareness	97
7-18	Common Words and Phrases to Reconsider	98
7-19.	The Ben Franklin Decision Tool	100
7-20.	Common Mistakes in Personal Improvement	101
	Takeaway Summary	102
8	**Time Management**	**103**
8-1.	Be a Hero: Save People Time!	103
8-2.	How to Easily Be 10 Percent More Productive Than Your Coworkers	104
8-3.	Urgency and Importance	105
8-4.	Balance in Life	105

8-5.	What Are Your Productive Times of Day?	106
8-6.	Respect Your Own Time	106
8-7.	Time *Is* Money!	106
8-8.	Time-Saving Filing Tip	108
8-9.	Dump, Delay, Do, or Delegate	108
8-10.	Common Mistakes in Time Management	108
	Takeaway Summary	108

9 A View of Corporate America — 111

9-1.	The Main Reason for This Chapter	111
9-2.	What Is "Corporate America"?	112
9-3.	Perceptions of Corporate America	112
9-4.	A Look at One Company in Corporate America	113
9-5.	Does Corporate America Rip You Off?	114
9-6.	Risk and Reward	115
9-7.	What Is Fair Compensation?	115
9-8.	"Your Fair Share"	116
9-9.	Greed and "Free"	117
9-10.	What Should Companies Do with Their Profits?	118
9-11.	If You Have a Complaint with a Company	118
9-12.	"Last Chance to Send $1!"	119
9-13.	Common Mistakes about Corporate America	119
	Takeaway Summary	119

10 Wealth and Finances — 121

10-1.	What Is Wealth?	122
10-2.	Wants vs. Needs	123
10-3.	Setting Your Wealth Bar	123
10-4.	How to Start Saving Money	124
10-5.	How to Increase Your Savings Account Balance Quickly	125
10-6.	Debt Reduction and Elimination	125
10-7.	Establishing Credit	126
10-8.	The Power of Compound Interest	126
10-9.	"But Later the Money Won't Be Worth Much!"	128
10-10.	Keep a Budget	128
10-11.	Budgeting Tools	129
10-12.	Key Ideas for a Budget	129

10-13. Learn Economics in One Short Lesson 132
10-14. Cash and Credit Card Management 134
10-15. Your Credit Report and Credit Score 135
10-16. Common Mistakes about Wealth, Finances, and Investing 135
        Takeaway Summary 135

11 Thinking of Your Own Small Business? 137
11-1.   Thinking of Starting Your Own Small Business? 138
11-2.   Naming and Branding Your Company 139
11-3.   Acquire Business Skills 139
11-4.   Focus: What Is Your Niche? 140
11-5.   Teamwork 140
11-6.   Profit: What It Is and What It's For 140
11-7.   Corporation, Sole Proprietorship, LLC, or DBA? 141
11-8.   Assorted General Ideas That (Eventually) Worked 141
11-9.   Assorted Custom-Programming Business Ideas
        That (Eventually) Worked 149
11-10. If You Want to Raise Your Rates 152
11-11. Common Mistakes in Starting and Running a Business 152
        Takeaway Summary 152

12 Dealing with a Mental Illness 155
12-1.   About Mental Illnesses 155
12-2.   Sidebar: What Makes Us Human? 158
12-3.   Sidebar: A Challenge to the Next Generation 159

13 Suggested Videos 161
13-1.   Emotional Intelligence 161
13-2.   Steve Jobs—Commencement Address at
        Stanford University, 2005 161
13-3.   Susan Cain—the Power of Introverts 162
13-4.   Dr. Kelly McGonigal—How to Make Stress Your Friend 162
13-5.   Overuse of Mobile Phones? 162
13-6.   A Magazine Is an iPad That Does Not Work 162
13-7.   Hans Rosling—Two Hundred Countries,
        Two Hundred Years 162
13-8.   Sir Harold Evans—Who Really Invented the Franchise? 163
13-9.   Monty Python—"The Argument Clinic" 163

14 Venturing Out   165
   14-1.   How Do You Proceed from Here?   165

References   167

About the Author   173

Foreword to the First Edition

Graduating from school and entering the "real world" is an extremely exciting time. After so many years of school, the idea of being free and venturing out on your own makes you exhilarated—and possibly nervous. From life's daily events, you will celebrate many great successes and also learn from many mistakes along the way. While school has prepared you for many of the challenges that lie ahead, there are many other important real-world lessons that you never learned in school. Most of us learn these lessons the hard way, wishing we had known the answers earlier, before we made mistakes. The lucky ones, however, will acquire much of this knowledge early on from a wise mentor. Consider yourself lucky, because in the pages that lie ahead you are about to learn many of life's important lessons from one of the wisest mentors I know.

I returned to college later in life, after many years of learning life's tough lessons on my own. I was fortunate enough to find myself in the classroom of Mr. David Kramer in the fall of 2013. It was clear from the start that he was different from any teacher I had ever worked with. In addition to covering the course material, Mr. Kramer frequently injected many important and practical lessons from his own life experiences. I put many of his teachings and ideas to use in my own life right away and greatly benefited from it. I consider Mr. Kramer to be a great mentor and a friend. Life would have been much easier if I had met him earlier in my journey, but I am forever grateful that our paths eventually crossed.

This book is your opportunity to learn some of life's most important lessons from a wise and successful mentor. You'll learn skills that will help you land your dream job, manage your finances, build wealth, and expertly manage your time. I wish I had learned many of these lessons twenty years ago. Fortunately, once you read this book, you won't have to say the same thing.

One of the many reasons we study history in school is to avoid making the same mistakes others made in the past. Embrace this opportunity to learn from the successes and failures of a dedicated teacher. My life is much better thanks to the teachings of Mr. Kramer, and I am confident that yours will be too. Enjoy *The Real World*!

Bruce Nault II
Denver, Colorado
May 2014

Foreword to the Second Edition

You are about to read a great book written by an influential teacher and mentor, who has learned through his own experiences how to be successful in all areas of life.

When I first found myself in an introductory computer science course, I was lost. With a background entirely rooted in social science, I'm not sure what was I thinking in trying to pursue computer science. Mr. Kramer was the best person to help guide me through this challenging course. His subtle humor and slight commentary helped keep things light as we dove into concepts I never thought I'd learn. Mr. Kramer is a unique teacher with a deeper understanding of his students' needs than most other teachers I've encountered. This was apparent right away. In each one of his classes, he gives one lesson of real world advice from this book, all of which he has learned through his own experiences. His willingness to be vulnerable and authentic with his students is something to be admired. One of Mr. Kramer's first pieces of advice was to find a mentor. I was lucky to find one in him. Computer science was a course that was outside of my area of expertise, but having a deeper connection with my teacher contributed to my success considerably.

I soon learned that Mr. Kramer and I have a lot in common! Both from the east coast, we somehow found our way to Colorado and eventually summiting many of the great 14,000-foot peaks that line the Colorado horizon. I mentioned that I also enjoy, and sometimes suffer through, the long treks up these mountains. Knowing he has summited all 54 of them gave me a new appreciation for all that Mr. Kramer has accomplished in his lifetime. He started giving me advice on how to best summit and I'd share my own experiences on the mountains. He even gave me a compass that had helped guide him up many of these treacherous peaks.

Mr. Kramer is a man with intention. He proceeds in a common sense fashion, with each step getting him closer to his goals. I'm sure this wasn't always the case, though through the years he has learned some strategies for achieving goals without making too many wrong moves. On a mountain peak, one wrong step could lead to devastating consequences. College students, on the other hand, seem to be galloping up the mountains, spinning, twisting, blindfolded, getting closer and closer to the top. Once they summit they're not sure which way to go.

Much like the compass Mr. Kramer gave me to help guide me on my challenging hikes, *The Real World* offers navigation for living well. Using his own experiences, he offers you strategies from interviewing to conflict resolution to starting your own business to managing mental illness. The pieces of advice you'll find in this book are relevant at any stage of your life. *The Real World* is like a trail map for succeeding outside the classroom and living with intention. Enjoy!

Nicole Beck
Denver, Colorado
December 2019

Acknowledgments

Family first. Thanks to my father and mother, Harold and Lucy Kramer, who by their example rather than their words showed me what is important in life: family, community, and friends. My grandfather, Aaron Joseph Sterman, demonstrated by example how important it is to be true to one's principles. Siblings Judy Chait, Chaim (Jesse) Kramer, and Lenny Kramer, and cousins Marge and Egon Berg, Mark and Suzanne Diskind, and Ted and Shosh Diskind, were there for me when I needed it most, helping me rebuild from episodes of bipolar disorder. And thanks to cousins Dr. Norman and Karolynn Coleman, and Dr. Arthur and Shelly Fierman—you know why.

Teachers next. Thanks to *all* my teachers, who, by choosing a profession that helps the next generation take its place in the world, enabled me to learn life skills and enjoy daily the benefits of their investment. A special thanks to two teachers whose lessons propel me every day, decades after our paths crossed: my master's thesis advisor, the late Professor Amir Pnueli of the Weizmann Institute of Science, whose humor and uncanny ability to see solutions to tough technical challenges inspired me; and my physics teacher, the late Professor Andrew J. Galambos, who enabled me to emerge from Flatland.

As the sayings go, "A friend is someone who knows all about you but likes you anyway" and "A friend is a relative you choose for yourself." For being there for me during my Triumphs and Disasters, thanks to Steven Bachrach,

Tom Lisjac, Catherine C. Loe, Krystyna Maliniak, Nino Posella, Jerry Rudisin, and Marshall Shapiro.

Thanks to my publisher, Rowman & Littlefield, for believing in this project, and especially to Dr. Tom Koerner, Carlie Wall, Christine Fahey, and the copyeditor, Scott Spillman, who provided this new author many ideas to improve this book.

Thanks to the Metropolitan State University of Denver's Department of Mathematical and Computer Sciences, whose faculty hired me to teach computer science for a year, which indirectly led to this book. Thanks to the reviewers of early versions of the manuscript, especially my students. They provided excellent feedback about what worked and what needed improvement: Dr. Diane Davis, Joshua-James Dixie, Luke Faulkner, Gwen Hoang, Robert Kupfner, Benjamin Mackay, Nicole Beck, and Rachel Martinez, with a special thanks to Bruce Nault II for his many insights. Other friends who provided timely and valuable feedback include Cheryl Cerell, Dr. Allison Friederichs, Chrissie Hodges, Carey Sanchez, Peter Hettinger, Joseph Agos, and Kathy Donnelly.

Lastly, thanks to my unrequested teacher, bipolar disorder, which taught me through mania and depression to accept people for who they are. Everyone has a story.

* * * * *

Introduction

WE ALL START OUT THE SAME

We are all born with zero knowledge and the capacity to learn. Would you like to learn how to enter the real world armed with valuable ideas? That's what this book is all about!

Though I learned many valuable ideas and lessons in college, almost none included how to interview, get great reference letters, save money, resolve conflicts, learn the lingo of the workplace, think for myself, communicate well with others, communicate well with myself (self-talk, defining my goals), and much more. *The Real World* contains more than 160 practical ideas and tools on these and many other topics useful to anyone in any major or profession.

I've read, seen, and heard scores of tools and techniques for self-improvement. The gist of these tools is that you can be anything you want to be and accomplish anything you want to accomplish, with which I wholeheartedly agree. However, I've also observed that most people

1. Still don't live the extraordinary lives depicted in common self-help tools
2. Work in jobs that are not their first choices for what they'd rather be doing

Sports heroes like Olympic athletes are powerful role models. But most people are not Olympic athletes and choose not to dedicate the time and energy that Olympians do. This book contains ideas that you can harness quickly and easily, one or two at a time, and that will provide positive outcomes quickly. I make no claims that using the ideas in this book will revolutionize your world or turn you into an Olympic athlete or millionaire. I *do* claim that the ideas in this book are quick and easy to apply on *your* road to *your* idea of success.

I live by a simple, one-level hierarchy of humanity—I don't rank or categorize people—and I respect an individual's right to choose his or her course of action as long as no one is harmed. The reason? Every one of us has his or her personal story of successes and failures, of victories and hardships. This book is a result of my own successes and failures in the form of ideas to enable you to succeed more easily.

If you dropped out of high school, didn't attend college, or didn't earn a degree, you'll find these ideas valuable, too, regardless of your interests. A college degree can certainly be a door opener, but it is not *necessary* to attain the successes you seek.

"If opportunity doesn't knock, build a door."

—*Milton Berle (1908–2002)*

I use many quotations throughout the book for two main reasons:

1. There are many people smarter and more experienced than I who emphatically or touchingly convey ideas and concepts better than I can.
2. Some ideas have been around for years, decades, centuries, or millennia. They just *appear* new because you may not have encountered them yet.

Out of respect for the authors, I quote passages exactly as they were written and don't "modernize" them to be gender neutral. I give the dates of birth (and death, if applicable) of most people I quote to demonstrate item 2 above, that some ideas truly have been known for a long time. To indicate dates in the "thousands of years ago" category, I use the abbreviations BCE and CE (not BC and AD), which stand for "before the Common Era" and "Common Era," respectively. (These are the standard abbreviations in fields such as archaeology and history.) So a date of 2,500 years ago would be roughly 500 BCE, and 1,800 years ago would be around 200 CE.

I use people's real names except when I obviously don't. ☺ What may not be obvious is that I sometimes change the gender of the people whose identity I choose to hide.

CREDIT FOR THE IDEAS IN THIS BOOK

Because I had to learn them before I could write about them, many of the ideas in this book are not original to me. I list the source of each idea when I know it. This allows me to give credit for the idea and allows you to look for more information if a particular topic interests you. I've had the great fortune of learning from a few teachers who made a major positive impact on my life, and to them I give a heartfelt thank you. Many of the unattributed ideas in this book came from my

- father and mother, Harold and Lucy Kramer;
- immediate and extended family;
- master's thesis advisor; and
- physics teacher.

Another "teacher" was and is my manic-depressive illness, also known as bipolar disorder. Through this condition, I became aware that everyone has a story and learned to thoroughly appreciate days when moods are normal.

HOW THIS BOOK EVOLVED

During the 2013–2014 school year, I taught computer science on a one-year contract at Metropolitan State University of Denver in Colorado. During some sessions that ended before the allotted time, I started presenting ideas to help students make the transition into the real world. Several students commented that the ideas were very helpful, so I continued the optional talks. I also offered one-hour presentations to all students in the Department of Mathematical and Computer Sciences, which were well received.

I felt that students and people who had not attended or completed college would also benefit from a book packed with simple, easy-to-apply ideas to help them transition into the real world. Designed in short sections suitable for mobile devices, this book can be read almost anywhere. Yes, the hardcopy is still available.

Enjoy your journey and best wishes for success!

David Kramer
Denver, Colorado
May 30, 2014

1

Entering the Real World

1-1. WELCOME!

The secret to life is that there is no secret to life. We are all born with zero knowledge and the capacity to learn. You are entering the real world—or will be soon—and the knowledge you acquire with this book will make your transition easier. For example:

What are some powerful interviewing techniques? See idea 5-1.

How do you get great reference letters? See idea 5-2.

How do you start building wealth even if you're in debt? See ideas 10-3 to 10-5.

Do you want to easily be 10 percent more productive than your co-workers? See idea 8-2.

Are you an introvert or an extrovert? Why is that important? See ideas 2-5 and 13-3.

Entering the Real World contains more than 160 practical ideas and tools for people launching into the real world out of college, community college, or high school. One goal of this book is for you to apply these ideas to your life right away and to have you thinking, "I'm glad I learned this *now* and not after twenty years!" Another goal is to challenge you to think for yourself by tackling the many rhetorical questions you will find throughout this book.

If you like an idea, great—use it! If not, don't. Even better, post an idea on the book's Facebook page, www.facebook.com/EnteringTheRealWorld, for your fellow readers to see. It is certainly OK to use an idea from a source even if you don't agree with everything else from that source. All the ideas in this book are useful to readers of any age, gender, race, religion, national origin, physical ability or disability, height, weight, marital status, financial status, veteran status, political leaning, and even allegiance in sports.

There are many quotations throughout this book that share the perspectives of other people. The quotations also show that some ideas have been around for a long time, even though you may be learning them only now, as you enter the real world.

"You have your way. I have my way. As for the right way, the correct way, and the only way, it does not exist."

—*Friedrich Nietzsche (1844–1900)*

In other words, each of us is an individual with his or her personal wants and goals.

1-2. HOW YOU WILL BENEFIT

Another of this book's objectives is to help the next generation—you!—take its place in the world. For the most part, elementary schools, high schools, and colleges prepare people academically but not practically for the real world. This book's perspective is that of a teacher *guiding* a student and not telling him or her what to do or claiming to know all the answers to every question. This book will

1. save you time in adjusting to and flourishing in the real world;
2. get you to your goals faster; and

3. help you avoid failures and emotional setbacks while learning how to navigate life.

Will you ever win an Olympic gold, silver, or bronze medal? While anyone can attain reasonable goals, realistically most people will *not* pursue them the way an Olympic champion does. But you still can compete with yourself. This book provides easy access to simple ideas that you can implement immediately and quickly give you results.

If using an idea from this book doesn't work out as desired, that just means you've learned something that doesn't work and can try a new approach. Someone once asked Thomas Edison why he kept going after ten thousand failed attempts to create the incandescent light bulb. He replied, "I have not failed. I have just found ten thousand ways that won't work."

1-3. HOW TO USE THIS BOOK

Read Material in Any Order

You can read the book cover to cover, or you can pick topics that interest you and read the corresponding chapters or sections. Use the detailed table of contents to select topics of interest. Some ideas build on earlier chapters, but most are self-contained. Where relevant, there are references to related sections and ideas.

Near the end of most chapters is a section titled "Common Mistakes in . . ." that chapter's topic. If you are in a hurry to avoid mistakes, read the "Common Mistakes" sections first.

If you didn't go to college, are still in high school, or dropped out of high school, read chapter 2, "If You Are Still in School," anyway. ☺

"In school, you're taught a lesson and then given a test. In life, you're given a test that teaches you a lesson."

—*Tom Bodett (b. 1955)*

Idea Numbers, "Takeaway," "Take Action!," and "Takeaway Summary"

Each main idea has a unique number for easy reference and, for the e-book, easy navigation. The idea number is "chapter number–idea number in that chapter." For example, 4-5 is the fifth idea in chapter 4. Many ideas end with a specific "Takeaway," which summarizes the key concept in that section. Some sections also encourage you to "Take Action!" *now* or to expand on the pre-sented idea. Use your mobile phone, index cards, or a computer file to record your ideas. You'll slowly build up a personal list of powerful ideas to refer to every day. Each chapter with "Takeaway" entries ends with a convenient summary of those items (called "Takeaway Summary") along with their idea numbers for easy reference.

If you purchased the e-book, you can search for the phrases:

* Takeaway   which gives you a section's key point; and
* Take Action!   which gives you actions you can take right now.

You will benefit a lot more from this book by actively working the "Take Action!" ideas than by just reading them.

About Searching the Internet

The Real World has many quality ideas in a limited space. If a particular topic opens your mind, search the Web for follow-on ideas using the references provided as a starting point. For example, chapter 7 discusses the highly per-sonal topics of self-esteem and self-talk and lists a few internet resources. If you don't like or aren't comfortable with the recommendations, do your own research to find others that suit you.

"Not all information on the internet is accurate."

—*Abraham Lincoln (1809–1865)*

Clearly, some of the information on the internet is reliable and some is bogus. Use your judgment, think for yourself, and research diligently. Check vendor, reader, or customer comments on products and services. If you have contact information, use it! Ask the contacts specific questions relevant to your situation:

1. How did the idea, product, or service help others?
2. What are some of its drawbacks? (Be wary if the answer is none. Some-thing that seems too good to be true usually is.)
3. Is the product or service worth the money? Why or why not?

It is usually better to ask these questions face-to-face or in a phone conversation (as opposed to by e-mail or text) because body and voice language often reveal the true answers.

Should You Buy or Rent Recommended Resources?

You'll find many of the references mentioned in this book at your public library. You can then check out (pun intended) a book, DVD, or other media before buying it. If your local library doesn't carry a particular reference, the library staff can usually search for it at other libraries across the United States and get it for you within a few days or weeks. At the Denver Public Library, this service is called "Interlibrary Loan" (ILL), but it might have a different name at your branch. This great service allows you to easily access media that are not available in your local library system.

Disclaimers

The short disclaimer version: you are responsible for anything you do as a result of reading this book.

The longer disclaimer version:

1. The ideas offered in this book work. If an idea sounds useful to you, great, but use it at your own risk. If you don't like an idea, don't use it. You can post other ideas that worked for you on the book's website or Facebook page for fellow readers to benefit.
2. Discussions of and references to bipolar disorder (also known as manic-depressive illness) and mental illness are from personal experience and are not intended to imply suggested treatments or expertise in psychological matters. Anyone who thinks he or she has a mental illness or knows someone who has one should contact professionals. The reference section includes resources for dealing with mental illnesses.

All internet links were valid when the book was written. They might have changed since then, so it is possible that some links will be broken.

Onward!

2

If You Are Still in School

"You are responsible for learning new skills and for your continuous education."

—Source: *www.thepeoplegroup.com*

Several skills can come in handy while you are still in school, but even if you have already left or dropped out of school, it is never too late to put these simple ideas into practice:

- Look for a career.
- Use your school's career and internship services.
- Prepare now for your entry into the real world:
  a. Develop an impressive resume.
  b. Build your people network.
  c. Build relationships with teachers and mentors.
  d. Create a job portfolio.
  e. Protect and back up your computer files.
- Set salary expectations.
- Work with different types of people (covered in more detail in chapter 6).
- Boost your vocabulary to make a good impression.
- Keep your social media footprint clean.
- Avoid common mistakes while still in school.

2-1. LOOKING FOR A CAREER?

If you are unsure of your career path, ask yourself two simple questions: "What would I do for free?" and "Can I make a living doing that?"

What you are passionate about—and therefore would do for free anyway—is what you will probably do best and enjoy most. A classic book on career selection is *Do What You Love, the Money Will Follow*, by Marsha Sinetar. Here are three other people's opinions on the proper attitude toward choosing a career:

"Do what you love to do and give it your very best. Whether it's business or baseball, or the theater, or any field. If you don't love what you're doing and you can't give it your best, get out of it. Life is too short. You'll be an old man before you know it."

—Al Lopez (1908–2005), baseball player and manager

"Don't aim for success if you want it; just do what you love and believe in, and it will come naturally."

—David Frost (1939–2013), journalist

"Energy and persistence conquer all things."

—Benjamin Franklin (1706–1790)

Be prepared for many jobs and more than one career. Your education until now may have prepared you for one career, but the marketplace and technology are changing so fast that new career opportunities continuously emerge in many professions.

* Takeaway	You'll spend much of your life at your job. Enjoy what you do!
* Take Action!	List three activities you would do for free. Are they potential careers? Why or why not?

2-2. USE YOUR SCHOOL'S CAREER AND INTERNSHIP SERVICES

Undergraduate schools and high schools have staff in career offices that maintain relationships with many local, regional, and national companies. Use these resources to get introduced to some companies. These companies also run job fairs at which you can meet recruiters and other human resources personnel to learn about their companies and job opportunities. If you are not yet looking for a job, attend anyway. You will get a feel for what companies are looking for and can practice interviewing skills.

Internships are another way to get a foothold in a company. Whether or not an internship is paid, you get valuable real-world working experience and get to prove yourself. Internships often lead to full-time job offers before or upon graduation.

* Takeaway	Your school's career and internship programs are valuable sources of advice.
* Take Action!	Speak to your school's career advisers today! Check out internship opportunities today!

2-3. START PREPARING NOW FOR THE REAL WORLD

Develop an Impressive Resume

"Impressive" here means "anything that increases your chances of getting an interview." Note that the purpose of the resume is to get you the interview; the purpose of the interview is to get you the job. Companies rarely fill jobs based only on resumes, without meeting the candidates. Strange things, resumes. In our society, it is considered bad manners to brag, but not on resumes!

There are thousands of ways to create this highly personal document. Robert Half International, a well-respected international job-placement company, has resume preparation tips at http://www.roberthalf.com/resume -tips. Another source is www.linkedin.com. Large companies use computers to scan for keywords that match a job description, so the actual resume format is not as crucial as the content when applying to these firms. Smaller companies, however, usually take a more personal approach, which makes format more important.

Here are some key items to include on all resumes:

1. Your contact information! You'd be surprised how many resumes don't have all of a person's contact information. For an e-mail address, consider getting your own domain with your name from www.godaddy.com, a popular and inexpensive site for registering domain names.

   Sidebar: Get high-quality business cards with your contact information. It's a professional way to exchange phone numbers and e-mail addresses with possible job contacts.

2. How your work enhanced the companies you worked with. That means focusing on specific results and not just listing what you did. For example, "Improved staff productivity by 40 percent within six months" says more than "Increased productivity in my department." (Naturally, you have to be able to back up your statements if asked.) In sales jargon, this is called "selling benefits, not features." People reading your resume should be able to easily and clearly understand how they and their company will benefit if they hire you. By describing benefits, you create clearer pictures of your talents in your readers' eyes.

3. What *specifically and uniquely* makes you stand out from other candidates? As with your work experience, list your strongest points first so you "hook" your readers into reading more. Many people write generic comments like "creative, hard worker, focused, team player." Differentiate yourself with unique (and true) descriptions.

As you develop your resume, read portions out loud to hear how the words do or do not flow together and to find awkward or incorrect phrases.

There are two basic types of resumes: chronological and functional. The former lists your experience and education in chronological order and is more common among people with short work histories. The latter lists specific tasks you performed (and, of course, how they specifically benefited the company) and is usually used by more experienced people to shorten their resumes or de-emphasize the chronology.

A third type of resume to consider is a "visual resume," especially if you are in a creative-arts field. This type of resume loses its effectiveness in this book's black-on-white text, so see examples in color by searching the internet for "visual resume."

* Takeaway	Accumulate experience outside of school to start building an impressive resume.
* Take Action!	Create a resume and get feedback from personal and professional sources who deal with resumes on a regular basis. Ask your college's or community college's career development center to review it. (They will usually do this at no charge.)

Develop an Impressive Cover Letter

Your cover letter should be clear and concise, and it should offer new information that is not on your resume. Indicate how your qualifications directly address specific job requirements by referring to items on your resume. Explain explicitly why hiring you will more than satisfy the job requirements. If you do not write explicitly, you are relying on readers to imagine what you mean rather than *telling* them what you mean.

In large companies, cover letters are also scanned by computer, so be sure to stock your letter with keywords. The hiring staff from smaller companies actually reads the cover letter, which means keywords are not as important as with large companies. Traditionally, the cover letter is up to one page long.

You can also get tips on writing cover letters from Robert Half International at http://www.roberthalf.com/cover-letter-tips or from www.linkedin.com.

Build Your People Network

The Merriam-Webster dictionary defines networking as "the exchange of information or services among individuals, groups, or institutions; *specifically*: the cultivation of productive relationships for employment or business."

Networking with others takes time to produce results, so begin *now*. Cultivate relationships with teachers and mentors. Ask them to introduce you to people they know in your industry (see idea 5-2 on getting great reference letters).

Consider joining some excellent sites for networking: www.LinkedIn.com, www.Indeed.com, and www.Meetup.com. As of this writing, both internal human resources departments and external organizations use LinkedIn and Indeed heavily to find candidates. Meetup promotes professional, hobby, and recreational groups that meet regularly. If you enjoy the outdoors, for example, join a local Meetup group that runs outdoor activities; you never know whom you may meet to expand your business network while enjoying yourself!

Internships are a popular way to get a foot in the door. Consider working for no monetary compensation just to get the experience. You get to meet people who might, in turn, move to other companies, which expands the potential number of places where you have contacts and can find a job. Your college career office or teachers in your department usually know whom to contact for internships.

* Takeaway	Networking takes time but opens doors; start now!
* Take Action!	Ask one teacher for an introduction to a company or organization for employment or an internship. Join LinkedIn and Meetup.

Build Relationships with Teachers

To build relationships with teachers, approach them and explain you'd like their mentorship as you prepare to enter the workplace. You should offer to do work for teachers in return, though most won't accept it. Examples include doing research for them on a particular topic or providing help with investigating a textbook a teacher or department might be considering. Or simply ask how you can be of help. Ask your newly found mentor for contacts in your industry.

* Takeaway	Find teachers who can be mentors.
* Take Action!	Decide now on one teacher you will ask to mentor you.

Create a Portfolio of Accomplishments

Take pride in your work! Create a folder (electronic, paper, or both) in which you keep schoolwork that has been graded excellent. A folder name like "My Next Steps to Success" or "My Next Steps to a Job" creates a positive, reinforcing mental image.

Over time, as you see for yourself how your work has improved and expanded, you will boost your self-esteem (more on self-esteem in idea 7-2). Compare work you did as a freshman with your work as a senior. At interviews, you will be able to demonstrate how you have progressed in critical thinking, organization, and, if appropriate, technical skills.

* Takeaway   Using a success folder builds material for job interviews.
* Take Action!   Start your success folder now and use it to save examples of your excellent work.

Protect and Back Up Your Computer Files

Back up your files!

One student lost *all* his data when his computer crashed two weeks before the end of a semester. Aside from needing to spend precious time breaking in a new computer, he also had to redo several assignments that were due by the end of the semester. Another student who followed the advice to back up his files had a more pleasant experience. He lost thousands of transactions—two weeks of data entry—at work when one of his servers crashed. After his panic subsided, he remembered that he had started an online backup service a few months earlier. He calmly and casually restored his data in a few minutes.

There are a few approaches to backing up files:

1. An online service ("back up to the Cloud"). This is the most useful option because:
    a. Files can be *automatically* backed up after you change them. You don't have to remember to back them up.
    b. You can back up and synchronize files across several devices. So if you own a computer, a mobile phone, and a tablet, backups are synchronized across all devices.
    c. Using the internet, you can access the files from anywhere.
    d. Recovery from a crash can be coordinated from anywhere via the internet.
    e. Even if your computers and other devices are destroyed in a fire, your data is still safe.
    f. Some services allow you to save previous versions of a file, so you can restore an earlier version if you don't like changes you've made.

        The risks with an online backup service are the same as with any use of the Cloud. Your data could be exposed to hackers, the backup service could go out of business, or the service could increase its rates undesirably fast.

As of this writing, popular automatic backup sites that charge an annual fee include www.Idrive.com and www.Carbonite.com. Other companies offer a variety of services that range from no cost up to $10 a month. No-charge services like www.Dropbox.com and Google Drive are available, but you have to remember to back up the files you change.

2. An external disk drive. Plug one into a USB port, do the backup, remove the drive, and store it in a protected place like a fireproof safe. Your files will be safe from hackers, but the downside of this approach is that you could lose your computer and your backup to theft, fire, flood, tornado, or other natural causes.

3. An image backup. The previous two approaches back up only your data files. The image approach backs up *everything*: the operating system, the installed programs, your files, your browser settings—yes, everything. To restore a crashed computer, simply copy the image back to a disk drive or boot your computer from the image. One well-known company that sells image-backup software is Acronis (www.acronis.com); it also offers backup services. The downside is that it takes time to produce an image, so you probably won't want to create an image backup every day. One approach is to create a full image backup every week or two and use an online service or external disk drive to back up daily work until the next time you create an image.

* Takeaway	Back up your files! Now!
* Take Action!	Investigate and subscribe to an online backup service. Now!

2-4. SET SALARY EXPECTATIONS

Learn where your career choice might lead financially. Robert Half International publishes salary guides for many professions at www.roberthalf.com/salary-guides. Another useful site for salary determination is salary.com/research/salary.

Because the cost of living varies from city to city, you should remember to compare these costs too. See money.cnn.com/calculator/pf/cost-of-living/ to compare costs in different cities.

* Takeaway   Know salaries in your profession in the cities where you want to live.
* Take Action!   Determine a realistic salary range for your (future) profession.

2-5. INTROVERTS AND EXTROVERTS

You will live and work with both introverts and extroverts. Why is that important? Because the current conception in our society is that extroverts dominate, yet one-third to one-half of all people are introverts. "How can introverts and extroverts live and work well together?" asks author Susan Cain in her book *Quiet*. Both personality types contribute to relationships and society in different ways. If you plan on having a career, getting married or living with a significant other, or having kids, then her nineteen-minute video, http://ed.ted.com/lessons/susan-cain-the-power-of-introverts, will open your eyes to the situations of often-overlooked introverts. For example, the current elementary and high school learning model is for kids to work in groups or "pods." But what if a child is introverted, prefers working alone, and does his or her best work alone? Sometimes that child is labeled "antisocial" or a "problem learner."

* Takeaway   Introverts and extroverts can work together productively while respecting each other's individuality.
* Take Action!   Watch Susan Cain's TED video.

2-6. BOOST YOUR VOCABULARY AND WRITING SKILLS

An expanded vocabulary and excellent writing skills are helpful both personally and professionally. Anyone you communicate with sees or hears thousands of messages a day. Make yours stand out with crisp vocabulary and clear, expressive writing.

There is no charge to join Wordsmith.org, which offers a new vocabulary word each workday and a recap on weekends. The site gives the word of the day's origins and earliest usage along with examples of usage and a quotation for the day. It's a fun way to boost vocabulary.

A classic book on writing is *The Elements of Style* by William Strunk Jr. and E. B. White. Cornell professor William Strunk had it privately printed in 1918 for his students' use. Mr. White, who studied under Professor Strunk, revised it and published the current edition in 1959. *Time* magazine recently picked *The Elements of Style* as one of the "100 best and most influential" nonfiction books written in English since 1923.

The book famously states, "Vigorous writing is concise."

* Takeaway	Stand out! Build a vocabulary and develop a writing style of your own.
* Take Action!	Subscribe to Wordsmith.org or find another "word a day" site and subscribe. Read *The Elements of Style*.

2-7. AVOID NEGATIVE OR QUESTIONABLE DIGITAL TATTOOS

A digital tattoo is what you leave whenever you use the Internet: consider your communication permanent and the trail of websites you visit viewable by anyone at any time. A potential employer will want to see your social media accounts. In other words, skip posting pictures of wild parties and evidence of outrageous pranks.

A website you can visit to help clean up your social media and keep them clean is the Delete Me tool on https://abine.com.

* Takeaway	Prevent questionable postings on your social media.
* Take Action!	Cleanse your social media accounts of postings that could interfere with finding a job (or significant other).

2-8. THE LOST ART OF TRUE BROWSING

When was the last time you opened a printed dictionary to look up a word? Today, you can google "define train" and immediately see various definitions of the word "train." (The Concise Oxford English Dictionary has six definitions each for "train" as a verb and as a noun.) But when you look up a word online, you don't get to see words before or after it, and you never stumble upon a word on a different page as you are looking for the word you want. If you insist on "browsing" online, visit www.StumbleUpon.com. It's like www .Pandora.com, but for the mind instead of for music. It enables you to easily browse through topics that interest you and be introduced to new ideas.

"There is no such thing as useless knowledge."

—*Lee Sterman (b. 1928)*

---

* Takeaway	Browse printed copies of sources to stumble upon new and unexpected knowledge.

2-9. LEARN FROM WHAT YOU HAVE ALREADY ACCOMPLISHED

A park ranger leading a tour in Yosemite Valley said, "Remember to turn around once in a while to enjoy the view from where you came." That comment also applies to life. Look back occasionally and give yourself credit for what you have accomplished so far! Though it's easy to focus on what didn't work, take time to focus on your successes and congratulate yourself. Review *how* you succeeded to become more aware of your strengths.

* Takeaway	Understanding what led to your successes helps you become aware of success-oriented techniques you have developed and may not be aware of.
* Take Action!	Write down three recent successes and the steps you took to attain them. Write down three recent failures and the steps you can take next time to prevent them from recurring.

2-10. COMMON MISTAKES WHILE STILL IN SCHOOL

Students:

1. Do not use their school's career and internship services.
2. Do not develop a folder with excellent materials to present to prospective employers.
3. Do not develop relationships with faculty who could provide references or be mentors.
4. Do not learn about personal financial management (see chapter 10).
5. Do not acquire people skills (see chapters 4 and 6).

TAKEAWAY SUMMARY

2-1. You'll spend much of your life at your job. Enjoy what you do!

2-2. Your school's career and internship programs are valuable sources of advice.

2-3. Accumulate experience outside of school to start building an impressive resume.

2-3. Networking takes time but opens doors; start now!

2-3. Find teachers who can be mentors.

2-3. Using a success folder builds material for job interviews.

2-3. Back up your files!

2-4. Know salaries in your profession in the cities where you want to live.

2-5. Introverts and extroverts can work together productively while respecting each other's individuality.

2-6. Stand out! Build a vocabulary and develop a writing style of your own.

2-7. Prevent questionable postings on your social media.

2-8. Browse printed copies of sources to stumble upon new and unexpected knowledge.

2-9. Understanding what led to your successes helps you become aware of success-oriented techniques you have developed and may not be aware of.

3

Think for Yourself

"A person with a new idea is a crank until the idea succeeds."

—Mark Twain (1835–1910)

The main ideas to consider while learning to think for yourself are how to do the following:

- Avoid categorizing people and recognize that each person has a history and a story.
- Recognize choice and opportunity in America.
- Express gratitude.
- Adopt a positive attitude.
- Live *your* life, not someone else's.
- Get mentors of all ages.
- Be intellectually honest.
- Acknowledge and accept ignorance and mistakes.
- Learn to follow the money when evaluating reports or news.
- Be careful with false alternatives.
- Be careful with statistics.
- Use failure as a learning tool.
- Avoid common mistakes while learning to think for yourself.

3-1. A JOY OF ADULTHOOD: THINKING FOR YOURSELF

A major joy of adulthood is that you get to think for yourself!

Relatively few events change the entire course of a life. Three of them are learning to walk, read, and drive. Learning to think for yourself is a fourth, but that typically is a process, not a one-time event. Until you learn to think for yourself, you are apt to react based on these quotes:

"You don't believe what you see. You see what you believe."

—Anonymous

---

and

"If you don't decide for yourself what you want, you'll live someone else's life."

—Anonymous

But as martial arts master Bruce Lee (1940–1973) said, "I'm not in this world to live up to your expectations, and you're not in this world to live up to mine."

One aspect of adulthood is being able to live with ambiguity. Entertainment media gets you used to quick resolutions. Problems on TV are usually resolved in 30 or 60 minutes. In real life, they often take much longer, and sometimes they're never resolved at all.

* Takeaway   Think for yourself and believe in yourself.
* Take Action!   Think for yourself!

3-2. DON'T CATEGORIZE PEOPLE; EVERYONE HAS A STORY

"All generalizations are false, including this one." ☺

—Mark Twain (1835–1910)

For the most part, generalizations about people are false. Each individual has a private, personal story about what got him or her to any point in life. So don't categorize people; look at them for who they are. Borrowing from the world of software programming, avoid "if . . . then . . . else" generalizations. An example of this is thinking, "If a person is a member of a certain political party, then he or she must also believe . . ." and fill in your favorite stereotype. Put another way:

"Do not judge your friend until you have put yourself in his place."

—*Hillel (first century BCE), Pirkei Avot 2:5*

And because you can *never* fully understand how people's situations affect them, do not *ever* judge anyone at all.

However, at least one generalization about people is true. Every nationality, race, religion, age group, country, profession, or any other group of people always includes both pleasant individuals and unpleasant individuals. But neither the former nor the latter defines the group.

"Once you label me you negate me."

—*Soren Kierkegaard (1813–1855), philosopher*

---

* Takeaway	Everyone has a unique story and background. Don't categorize people.
* Take Action!	Think of a friend or relative you judged negatively and ask yourself if your conclusions were appropriate.

3-3. CHOICE AND OPPORTUNITY IN AMERICA

One of the many great things about America is that you get to *choose* your destiny without regard to gender, race, color, creed, religion, age, or the happiness or unhappiness of your childhood.

Some people have excruciatingly difficult obstacles to overcome, but even people who face difficult obstacles still get to choose their destiny. Fortunately, choice is always present, whether that choice involves going from rags to riches, going from riches to rags, or simply writing a term paper on time. You choose to write the paper or not, and you face the outcome either way.

To see fascinating people creating fascinating opportunities in America, watch the TV show *Shark Tank*. Entrepreneurs from all walks of life present their business opportunities to a panel of potential investors. It is a penetrating glimpse at American ingenuity, initiative, and choice in action.

Another example of choice is your reaction to advertising. One goal of all advertising is to convert "wants" to implied "needs." Advertisers try to convince you that their product will raise your self-esteem, make you a better person, and enrich you beyond your wildest dreams. You can *choose* to let those messages go right by you and not be sucked into believing you have less or are less of a person.

* Takeaway	America is still the land of choices.
* Take Action!	List three things you feel you *have* to do and the choices you can make to do something more beneficial instead. For example, do you *have* to go to that concert tonight, or can you *choose* to complete an assignment that is due tomorrow? (See idea 10-2.)

3-4. GRATITUDE

It's easy to dwell on what you don't have. Be grateful instead for what you *do* have. Here's a reminder that even math-phobics can use to express gratitude: $f = 10$.

In this equation, f stands for "fingers." Most people have ten fingers, ten toes, two eyes, and the common number of everything else. Those who don't have the common numbers have difficulties often overlooked or not seen by those who do. Be grateful for your health and remind yourself to express your gratitude daily with $f = 10$ (or your equivalent), because life would be much less comfortable with $f = 9$, $f = 4$, or $f = 0$.

* Takeaway

"Learn how to be happy with what you have while you pursue all that you want."

—*Jim Rohn (1930–2009)*

"Be careful what you ask for; you might get it."

—*Anonymous*

*Take Action!   Write three situations you're grateful for and use
                       one to create your own version of a daily $f = 10$.

3-5. IT'S TRUE! A POSITIVE ATTITUDE HELPS!

Another path toward thinking for yourself is your attitude. It is easy to have
a positive attitude about successes, but failures and problems pose greater
challenges. During the 1964 Olympics, Jimmie Heuga (1943–2010) became
one of the first two Americans ever to medal in skiing. He contracted multiple sclerosis in 1970, ending his skiing career. But he maintained a positive
attitude by keeping his problems in perspective: "You think I have problems?
I just have multiple sclerosis. . . . Some people can't balance a checkbook!"

A positive attitude provides the stimulus to get yourself past problems by
enabling you to focus on solutions and future goals. Figure skater Scott Ham-
ilton (b. 1958), winner of four consecutive U.S. and World championships
and a gold medalist in the 1984 Olympics, put it this way: "The only disability
in life is a bad attitude."

And lastly, William James (1842–1910), a philosopher and the first educator to offer a psychology course in America, wrote: "The greatest discovery of
my generation is that a human being can alter his life by altering his attitude."

* Takeaway   A positive attitude helps celebrate successes and
                       surmount difficulties.
* Take Action!   Think of a time you had a negative attitude about
                       something that didn't turn out well for you. What
                       can you do differently next time?

3-6. LIVE *YOUR* LIFE, NOT SOMEONE ELSE'S

Here are five quotations from a source to be mentioned in a moment:

1. "I wish I'd had the courage to live a life true to myself, not the life others
   expected of me."
2. "I wish I didn't work so hard."
3. "I wish I'd had the courage to express my feelings."
4. "I wish I had stayed in touch with my friends."
5. "I wish that I had let myself be happier."

The quotes are from the book *The Top Five Regrets of the Dying: A Life Transformed by the Dearly Departing*, by Bronnie Ware, an Australian woman who has worked with hospice patients. (A hospice is a home or program that provides care for the sick or terminally ill.) They are composite quotes from people she has cared for. She writes about the first one (with Australian spelling):

> This was the most common regret of all. When people realise that their life is almost over and look back clearly on it, it is easy to see how many dreams have gone unfulfilled. Most people had not honoured even a half of their dreams and had to die knowing that it was due to choices they had made, or not made.

See http://www.hospicepatients.org/five-regrets-of-the-dying-bronnie -ware.html for more on this topic.

* Takeaway	Live *your* life, not someone else's, starting *now*.
* Take Action!	Write two ways you are living someone else's life and what you can do to change that starting *now*.

3-7. FIND MENTORS OF ALL AGES

Find mentors whom you admire and respect. Ask them about how they succeeded, coped, improved, helped others, learned from failure, or saved money, among other things. Remember, everyone starts with zero knowledge, so they had to accumulate theirs, too. There are many people who are happy to share their acquired knowledge and experiences with you. While in the real world, you will come in contact with many outstanding men and women. Invite some of them to lunch (pay for it!) and ask how they learned to deal with success and failure. Having mentors of different ages also helps you prepare for the different stages of your life.

Are there people, past or present, whom you admire? Learn about them and how they attained their successes, recovered from failures, and lived their lives. Read their biographies, search the internet for stories and videos about them, and learn what they did that helped them reach their goals. Adopt what you are comfortable with.

For example, Lee Iacocca (1924–2019) turned a failing Chrysler Corporation around in 1979. He writes in his autobiography: "No one ever lay on his deathbed saying I could have closed one more sale." That puts many things into perspective to help you decide what is truly important and what is merely urgent (more on importance and urgency in idea 8-3).

* Takeaway	Find mentors of all ages to help you prepare for all of life's stages.
* Take Action!	Ask one person to be a mentor. He or she can be a teacher, a coworker at a higher level, or someone in your future profession.

3-8. INTELLECTUAL HONESTY

Intellectual honesty (a concept emphasized by Andrew J. Galambos in his courses; see www.fei-ajg.com) is keeping your mind open to ideas that challenge your beliefs. An open mind is not as common as it sounds. (Idea 4-5 discusses how the masses think.)

* Takeaway	"If nothing else in life, I want to be true to the things I believe in, and quite simply, to what I'm all about. I know I'd better, because it seems whenever I take a false step or two, I feel the consequences."
	—*Peyton Manning (b. 1976)*
* Take Action!	Dig down deep about something you know you are not being honest about with yourself. Write two reasons why you continue to be dishonest with yourself and two ways to change that.

3-9. "I DON'T KNOW" AND "I MADE A MISTAKE"

An offshoot of intellectual honesty is admitting to yourself "I don't know" and "I made a mistake" when appropriate. These acknowledgments are the gateway to learning and expanding knowledge.

* Takeaway	"Being ignorant is not so much a shame, as being unwilling to learn."
	—*Benjamin Franklin (1706–1790)*

* Take Action!   Write down a mistake that you recently made but
                        later denied making (to others or yourself). Say, "I
                        made a mistake!" out loud and with feeling to hear
                        for yourself that you can make mistakes and still
                        live. ☺

3-10. EXAMPLES TO CHALLENGE YOUR THINKING FOR YOURSELF

Who Are Your Friends and Why?

Whom do you call a friend?

"A friend is one before whom I may think aloud."

—*Ralph Waldo Emerson (1803–1882)*

Do you feel this way about *all* the people you call your friends, close or otherwise? As you think more for yourself, you'll see more clearly before whom
you can think aloud. Which friends respect your time, encourage your goals,
and genuinely help you feel better about yourself? Which "friends" scoff at
your life plans, discourage you from seeking your goals, or leave you feeling
sad, annoyed, or angry when you spend time with them?

Consider "firing" some of these supposed "friends." Are there people
you've been pursuing as friends or for romantic involvement who don't want
anything to do with you? Mentally fire them! Don't tell them you're firing
them, just phase out your contact with them. Why waste time on relationships that are going nowhere or cause you to feel worse about yourself?

* Takeaway   You may have outgrown people you consider your
                      friends.
* Take Action!   "Fire" the "friends" who drag you down.

How Did You Arrive at Your Political Views?

In the real world, you will encounter people from all walks of political life.
What are your own political views, and why? Have you thought through your
beliefs, or are you parroting what you've been told or what you've heard over
and over again? Here are a few questions to ponder:

1. What is it about America that still makes it the number one country that people around the world want to immigrate to?
2. What made America the great country it is and how can you tell? What is the source of the information you rely on? By the way, what does "great" mean? (More on defining terms in idea 4-2.)

Politicians talk about concepts like "progress," "fair," "profit," "equality," "racism," and, well, throw in your favorite terms. For each of these words, ask yourself the following questions:

1. What does the word mean to you?
2. What does the word mean to all Americans?
3. How can you determine what that word means to all Americans?
4. How do politicians determine what that word means to all Americans?

Take a word like "progress." One person's progress could be another person's demise. A classic example is a horse-and-buggy manufacturer observing the "horseless carriage"—yes, the car—emerging onto the American scene in the early 1900s. Another example is America's extraordinary interstate highway system, begun in the 1950s. Cities and towns that were awarded exits on the highways experienced growth. Those in between exits did not—and, in some cases, dried up as a result. But the highway system was labeled "progress."

* Takeaway	Understand how you arrived at your political views. Think for yourself and do your own open-minded research.
* Take Action!	Assume for a moment the point of view of an opposing political party. Understand why and how people believe that party's views.

A Lighter Side of Conservatives and Liberals

Speaking of politics, are you a conservative, liberal, or neither? One definition of a conservative is "a liberal with two teenage daughters."

Now meet the satirist Ambrose Bierce (1842–ca. 1913). His humorous definition of a conservative shows that not much has changed since his day:

"Conservative, *n*: A statesman who is enamored of existing evils, as distinguished from the Liberal who wishes to replace them with others."

Bierce's *Devil's Dictionary* has scores of amusing definitions, like "Sweater, *n*: garment worn by child when its mother is feeling chilly."

3-11. FOLLOW THE MONEY

Have you ever seen a report by supposedly "impartial, objective experts" like scientists, doctors, economists, or psychiatrists? (Or pick your favorite profession.) Find out who paid for the report and you'll probably find the real—that is, hidden—reasons behind its conclusions. Consider reports on topics such as the economy and health care. Who paid for the reports? What are their political, economic, and social agendas? How impartial and objective do you think they really are? And, of course, how do the authors know they are right? (See idea 4-3 for a discussion on how you know you are right.)

* Takeaway	Follow the money that created a report and look at all sides of a topic. Think for yourself!
* Take Action!	Examine reports whose conclusions you agree with and reports whose conclusions you disagree with. Follow the chain back to who paid for the reports and determine whether your opinions still hold.

3-12. BE CAREFUL WITH FALSE ALTERNATIVES

"Do you want your new car in red, or do you want it in blue?"

A false alternative is a proposed selection between one or more choices, none of which is desired, relevant, or maybe even possible. The question above is a takeoff on the kind of pressure a car salesperson might use to force a decision on a sale. False alternatives are common in advertising and politics, so always look for additional options. In relationships experiencing conflict, sometimes a false alternative is offered in the heat of an argument. Here are simplistic examples to illustrate false alternatives and demonstrate helpful responses:

FRIEND 1:	Either we talk now or I leave.
FRIEND 2:	I'd like some time to collect my thoughts.

Or at work:

STAFF MEMBER 1:	Either we use my approach or I quit the project.
STAFF MEMBER 2:	Has the team considered other approaches?

* Takeaway	False alternatives often mask many reasonable, un-mentioned alternatives.

3-13. BE CAREFUL WITH STATISTICS

A spin-off of following the money and false alternatives is to be careful with statistics. For example, it's been said that 86.4 percent of all statistics are false. Or is it 84.6 percent? ☺

Here's a way that simple statistics can twist a situation: if one person earns $100,000 a year and another person earns $0 a year, their average income is $50,000. Hey, that's not bad! (Tell that to the person earning $0.)

Do you ever hear a newscaster say, "A report says that the majority of Americans prefer . . ."? What you may not know is that the study showed only 50.0001 percent of Americans have that preference!

* Takeaway	A table of numbers or a set of graphs might look "impressive," "good," and "official," but always check the source and spot-check the data.
* Take Action!	The next time someone presents you with statistics (fishy or otherwise), determine the source of the data.

3-14. FAILURE AS A LEARNING TOOL

Embrace failure as a learning tool. Henry Ford (1863–1947), who created the Model T automobile and the Ford Motor Company, once wrote, "Failure is the opportunity to begin again more intelligently." There is extensive media coverage on success in American society—in the sports and entertainment industries, for example—but little on the fact that there are often many failures before one success.

If you're always trying your best and things don't work out as you hoped, you can choose to focus on the failure or you can treat the experience as a learning opportunity. Some people who experienced various degrees of failure before success include:

1. Theodor Geisel (Dr. Seuss) had twenty-seven publishers reject his first book, *And to Think That I Saw It on Mulberry Street*.
2. J. K. Rowling went in five years from being a penniless, depressed, divorced single parent attending school to publishing her first *Harry Potter* book.
3. Michael Jordan was cut from his high school basketball team.
4. Walt Disney was fired by a newspaper editor because "he lacked imagination and had no good ideas." After that, Disney started several businesses that failed before a mouse changed the world.

If you get turned down for a job, reflect on what you can do to improve your chances for success the next time. One approach is to contact the person who delivered the news and ask why the company chose another candidate. Some people are reluctant to respond because they are concerned you might sue them. But others can offer valuable comments on why you were not selected.

* Takeaway	It's not failure if you don't achieve a goal but learn what to do next time. It's failure only if you don't learn from it or stop trying.
* Take Action!	Write down three times you recently failed to achieve a goal, no matter how big or small. For each one, list the reason(s) you didn't reach the goal and what you learned from the failure to improve your chances for success next time.

3-15. TWO POEMS FOR TOUGH TIMES

How do you react to tough times? Two poems will help you through them and enable you to stay away from the "why me?" trap:

"If," by Rudyard Kipling (1865–1936)

"How Did You Die?" by Edmund Vance Cooke (1866–1932)

One stanza in "How Did You Die?" stands out:

> Oh, a trouble's a ton, or a trouble's an ounce,
> Or a trouble is what you make it,

And it isn't the fact that you're hurt that counts,
But only how did you take it?

You *can* choose whether a problem weighs a ton or an ounce, and how to deal with it.

* Takeaway	You can choose how to respond to a problem. You can choose "an ounce" of temporary distraction or "a ton" of wallowing.
* Take Action!	Look up the two poems on the internet and read them.

3-16. COMMON MISTAKES WHILE LEARNING TO THINK FOR YOURSELF
People:

1. Continue to categorize other people.
2. Fail to speak up as a kid or young adult to discuss life's major questions. They suppress nagging questions for fear of upsetting others.
3. Don't look at issues with intellectual honesty and suppress what their gut is telling them.
4. Maintain predetermined opinions instead of examining all sides of an issue.

TAKEAWAY SUMMARY
3-1. Think for yourself and believe in yourself.

3-2. Everyone has a unique story and background. Don't categorize people.

3-3. America is still the land of choices.

3-4. "Learn how to be happy with what you have while you pursue all that you want."

3-4. "Be careful what you ask for; you might get it."

3-5. A positive attitude helps celebrate successes and surmount difficulties.

3-6. Live *your* life, not someone else's, starting *now*.

3-7. Find mentors of all ages to help you prepare for all of life's stages.

3-8. "If nothing else in life, I want to be true to the things I believe in, and quite simply, to what I'm all about. I know I'd better, because it seems whenever I take a false step or two, I feel the consequences."

3-9. "Being ignorant is not so much a shame, as being unwilling to learn."

3-10. You may have outgrown people you consider your friends.

3-10. Understand how you arrived at your political views.

3-10. Think for yourself and do your own open-minded research.

3-11. Follow the money that created a report and look at all sides of a topic. Think for yourself!

3-12. False alternatives often mask many reasonable, unmentioned alternatives.

3-13. A table of numbers or a set of graphs might look "impressive," "good," and "official," but always check the source and check the data.

3-14. It's not failure if you don't achieve a goal but learn what to do next time. It's failure only if you don't learn from it or stop trying.

3-15. You can choose how to respond to a problem. You can choose "an ounce" of temporary distraction or "a ton" of wallowing.

4

Communicating with Others and Yourself

"More people in the world have mobile phones than toilets."

—Source: *https://www.buzzfeednews.com/article/jessicamisener*

The main ideas to consider while learning to communicate with others and yourself are how to do the following:

- Get your point across quickly to any audience.
- Say what you mean and define your terms.
- Know whether you are right or wrong.
- Distinguish between facts and opinions.
- Deal with the opinions of the masses.
- Identify who is responsible for solving a problem.
- Recognize who has the risk in an outcome.
- Approach relationships.
- Resolve conflicts.
- Look people in the eye.
- Keep your social media presence clean.
- Avoid common communication mistakes.

4-1. GET YOUR POINT ACROSS IN THIRTY SECONDS OR LESS

Read *How to Get Your Point Across in 30 Seconds or Less* by Milo O. Frank (b. 1928). Learn the five key approaches for communicating your ideas quickly and efficiently. By the way, it's a short book. ☺

* Takeaway	You *can* get your points across quickly.
* Take Action!	Read *How to Get Your Point Across in 30 Seconds or Less*.

4-2. WHAT DO YOU MEAN? DEFINE YOUR TERMS

Defining your terms with semantic precision sends a powerful message to yourself and to those you associate with. Here are some words you hear every day: "success," "right," "wrong," "fair," "progress," "privacy," "deserve," "privileged," "common sense," "forever," "profit," and, of course, "normal." Take the word "success." What does success mean to you? To your boss? To your husband, wife, boyfriend, girlfriend, parents, children, or friends? Are these people's views about success harmonious with yours?

When you see financial reports released by a company or the government, what does "adjusted for inflation" mean? Adjusted *how*? Is inflation the only category that should be considered when comparing figures from years or decades ago? How about considering buying power, as in the number of work hours needed to buy a pound of kumquats, a refrigerator, a car, or a house?

The point: define your terms, at least to yourself. If you don't define "success" for yourself, for example, others will define it for you, and you'll pursue *their* goals, not yours. Or you'll have only a vague idea of where you're headed. Look at the wide variation in just four of the many possible definitions of success:

1. From Google, after googling "define success": "the accomplishment of an aim or purpose."
2. From the Merriam-Webster dictionary: "(1) the fact of getting or achieving wealth, respect or fame; (2) the correct or desired result of an attempt."
3. From Dr. Denis Waitley: "the attainment of a worthwhile goal" (note that "worthwhile" can also mean many different things to different people)
4. Based on a poem by Bessie A. Stanley (1879–1952):

To laugh often and much;
to win the respect of intelligent people and the affection of children;
to earn the appreciation of honest critics and endure the betrayal of
    false friends;
to appreciate beauty, to find the best in others;
to leave the world a bit better, whether by a healthy child, a garden
    patch or a redeemed social condition;
to know even one life has breathed easier because you have lived.
This is to have succeeded.

So what does success mean to *you*? Define it for yourself, or others will define it for you. Think of people—past or present—whose concept of success is compatible with yours. Learn about them, how they overcame obstacles, if possible talk to or e-mail them, and hear how they persisted until they attained their successes.

Credit for the importance of defining terms and the importance of semantic precision goes to Andrew J. Galambos. The course V-50DD discusses semantic precision in detail in Module 1. See http://www.fei-ajg.com/v-50courseinfo.html.

* Takeaway	Define clearly for yourself the important words that shape your future.
* Take Action!	Write out what you mean by the words listed at the start of this section: "success," "right," "wrong," "fair," "progress," "privacy," "deserve," "privileged," "common sense," "forever," "profit," and "normal." Think of other words or phrases that often lead to ambiguity or arguments, and define them for yourself. Discuss your list with your friends or coworkers and see how different the definitions are!
	See examples of semantic precision in the *Thrust for Freedom* pamphlets from the Free Enterprise Institute at http://www.fei-ajg.com/otherprintedit ems.html.

Example: What Is Progress?

Be careful with words that imply one thing but mean another, as they can create wrong perceptions. For example, the word "progress" means different things to different people. As a noun:

1. Oxford English Dictionary: "forward or onward movement toward a destination."
2. The Free Dictionary (online): "steady improvement, as of a society or civilization."
3. Merriam-Webster: "the process of improving or developing something over a period of time."

As a verb:

1. Oxford English Dictionary: "to move forward or onward in space or time."
2. The Free Dictionary (online): "to advance toward a higher or better stage; improve steadily."
3. Merriam-Webster: "to improve or develop over a period of time."

But what does "forward," "improvement," "better," or "higher stage" mean? From whose perspective? Do the definitions accommodate:

1. Horse-and-buggy drivers around 1900, before the automobile "progressed" them out of existence?
2. The use of computers to replace (displace) people?
3. Customers of the chain of stores called Blockbuster?
4. The technological differences between societies in the years 1000 and 2000?

Example: What Are Capitalism, Communism, and Socialism?

What's a better, more successful economy for society: capitalism, socialism, or communism? How do you know? What do *you* mean by these words? What do "better" and "successful" mean? Who decides for the populace? How?

The Oxford English Dictionary's definitions of the three terms are:

Capitalism	"An economic and political system in which a country's trade and industry are controlled by private owners for profit, rather than by the state."
Socialism	"1. A political and economic theory of social organization that advocates that the means of production, distribution, and exchange should be owned or regulated by the community as a whole. 2. Policy or practice based on the political and economic theory of socialism. 3. (in Marxist theory) A transitional social state between the overthrow of capitalism and the realization of communism."
Communism	"A political theory derived from Karl Marx, advocating class war and leading to a society in which all property is publicly owned and each person works and is paid according to their abilities and needs."

Which of these forms is present in America now? Does it matter? (Hint: yes.) How do you know? What is better for America? How do you know?

4-3. HOW DO YOU KNOW YOU ARE RIGHT?

Question: How do you know you are right?

This short question is one of the most profound ones you'll ever encounter in your *entire* life. This question is critical because it paves the way to thinking for yourself, as discussed in chapter 3. On what basis do you decide that you are right or wrong about anything? How do the people you associate with know they are right about their opinions? Can you distinguish among opinion, fact, and proof? How does this impact knowing if you are right about anything or not?

The philosopher René Descartes (1596–1650) said, "I think, therefore I am." Or, in the original Latin, *cogito ergo sum*.

A common view today is: "I think, therefore I am right."

Think about it. Where does everything you believe come from? Do you think for yourself or follow others? *How* do you decide what you believe?

Think for yourself, or others will be glad to think for you (and possibly penalize you if you disagree).

Pause here to let the question "How do you know you are right?" and its implications sink in.

As an example, the Social Security Act was passed in America in 1935 to create the Social Security system. Is it successful? Regardless of your opinion or political views, *how* do you know whether Social Security is successful? What does "successful" mean here? Is it a system that can survive? Regardless of your opinion, how do you know you are right?

People often adopt beliefs this way:

"A long habit of not thinking a thing wrong, gives it a superficial appearance of being right."

—*Thomas Paine (1737–1809)*

Credit goes to Andrew J. Galambos for expounding on the idea of how you know you are right. See www.fei-ajg.com/V-50courseinfo.html. The course V-50DD discusses this important concept in Module 1, Session 2.

* Takeaway	Answering "How do I know I am right?" on any subject helps you clarify your thoughts and proceed to your goals.
* Take Action!	Answer for yourself the difference between opinion, fact, and proof. For more information on this critical topic, see V-50DD, Module 1, Session 2. http://www.fei-ajg.com/v-50courseinfo.html.
* Take Action!	Write down three controversial topics and the view you currently hold on each of them. Ask and answer "How do I know I'm right?" for each of them.

4-4. ALL FACTS ARE OPINIONS; NOT ALL OPINIONS ARE FACTS

Recognize that anything anyone tells you about any topic is an opinion (including this entire book). But only some opinions are supported by fact. So all facts are opinions, but not all opinions are facts.

The statement "2 + 2 = 4" is an opinion that is a fact.

The statement "2 + 2 = 5" is an opinion that is not a fact.

Implicit at the end of every person's statement is the phrase "in my opinion." For example, if an economic "expert" says, "The economy is definitely improving" or "The economy is definitely worsening," add the phrase "in my opinion" to that sentence. How does that person know if he or she is right?

* Takeaway	All facts are opinions; not all opinions are facts.
* Take Action!	Explain all sides of a recent argument or disagreement you had (with yourself or others) and determine which facts support each side.

4-5. WHEN ARE THE MASSES RIGHT?

The masses are usually wrong. (That's an opinion. ☺) For example, what is the difference in the masses' beliefs about our planet in the years 1492, 1610, and now? Andrew J. Galambos gave these examples of the thinking of the masses:

1492	Columbus sails to America and back. The masses still believe Earth is flat.
1610	Using a telescope, Galileo Galilei is the first known person to see Jupiter's moons. The masses still believe the flat Earth is the center of the universe and the sun goes around Earth.
Now	Of *course* the Earth is round! Everybody knows that!

Not everybody. Visit www.TheFlatEarthSociety.org. The following was considered heresy in the 1600s:

"The Milky Way is nothing else but a mass of innumerable stars planted together in clusters."

—Galileo Galilei (1564–1642)

Here's a point to ponder: How do the masses eventually come to accept "heresies"? What are some beliefs that the masses accept today that will be laughed at in five hundred years like the flat Earth? In one hundred years? Fifty years? *Five* years from now? (Example: consider the latest fad diet, whatever it is.) Bottom line: think for yourself.

* Takeaway   Two quotes summarize these thoughts:

"Whenever you find yourself on the side of the majority, it is time to pause and reflect."

—*Mark Twain (1835–1910)*

"Time makes more converts than reason."

—*Thomas Paine (1737–1809)*

4-6. "WHOSE PROBLEM IS IT?"

One way to filter out problems presented to you is to ask, "Whose problem is it?" Then ask, "Whose problem is it to *solve*?"

For example, at a local Denver university, liberal-arts majors—some of whom truly hate math—are required to take a math course. Almost without fail, at the start of every semester, two or three students ask to speak privately with the instructor to say something like this: "I graduate at the end of this semester and have put off taking this course mostly out of fear and dread of math. I *have* to graduate!"

Whose problem is it? Not the teacher's! Whose problem are the students trying to make it? The instructor's! Whose problem is it to solve? The students'.

The message is *not*, "Don't help people solve their problems." The message is, "Help people solve their problems if the situation calls for it, but not when it is best for them to solve their problems on their own."

* Takeaway   Recognize and separate what are your or others' problems to solve.

* Take Action!   Think of two times when you assumed responsibility for someone else's problem when it was really that person's responsibility to solve. Write down what you will do the next time a similar situation occurs.

4-7. ABRAHAM LINCOLN AND THE COW'S TAIL

This story is attributed to Abraham Lincoln while Mr. Lincoln debated a political opponent:

LINCOLN: How many legs does a cow have?

OPPONENT: Four.

LINCOLN: If you call a cow's tail a leg, how many legs does a cow have?

OPPONENT: Why five, of course!

LINCOLN: No. Calling a cow's tail a leg does not make it a leg.

People commonly call concepts by different names, whether intentionally or unintentionally. Examples of words used and what they really mean:

Free	Eventually paid for by you or someone else
Free sample	A sample that you or someone else pays for indirectly
Investment	Expense or speculation
Need	Want
* Takeaway	Be careful to use or interpret the correct meaning of words so you don't mislead people or mislead yourself.
* Take Action!	Think of two situations that resulted in conflict or failure because you thought (symbolically) that calling a cow's tail a leg made it a leg. What will you do differently the next time that happens?

4-8. WHO HAS THE RISK IN AN OUTCOME?

Related to the question "Whose problem is it?" is another one posed by Andrew J. Galambos: "Who has the risk in the outcome?" If your boss tells you, "This project must be completed in four weeks!" who has the risk and potential loss if it isn't completed in four weeks? You? Your boss? Both of you? Someone else?

If someone has no risk in the outcome, weigh carefully what you do based on any advice, commands, instructions, or guidance you get from him or her.

Examples: What risk does a weather forecaster have in the outcome of the forecast? What risk do lawmakers have when they pass laws on a city, state, or federal level? Aside from reputation, the answer to both questions is *none*.

* Takeaway	Weigh carefully any advice given by people with no stake in the outcome.

4-9. SHOULD YOU WRITE, CALL, MEET, E-MAIL, TEXT, SEND A VIDEO?

With so many communication options available, should you write, call, e-mail, meet with, or send a text or video to a business or personal contact? It depends. Communicating with someone is highly personal, and different people and different circumstances call for different forms of communication. Direct interaction (meeting or calling) when getting to know someone is usually the most helpful option for several reasons:

1. You get to know the person and not the facade that e-mail, text, and video provide.
2. Body language, voice changes, and eye contact (on both sides of the conversation) tell a lot.
3. With an interactive exchange, you can ask and answer questions based on how the conversation develops. Indirect exchanges like e-mail and text don't provide that opportunity.

Clearly, communication is a two-way street, so take into account what is best for the person you want to communicate with. In business, it's sometimes hard to get people's attention to begin with. The following technique works well in some situations. If you don't get a response to a phone message, send a short e-mail (two or three sentences) indicating why you've been trying to contact that person. End the e-mail with something like, "I'll call you Tuesday at 2 p.m. to discuss this further if you're free." Placing the idea in the person's mind that you will call at a specific time often works. Notice that "if you're free" shows that you are considerate of the person's time and have no presumption he or she will talk with you.

Some people are more direct or blunt. Try different approaches and see what works comfortably for you. Be prepared to emerge from your comfort zone or you will make no progress. Remember that different people probably require different approaches.

What about your wording in an e-mail? Write in language that you'd feel comfortable showing your grandmother.

Finally, *always* write the "To:" part of an e-mail last. This serves two purposes: in emotionally charged situations, you give yourself space to reflect on whether you really want to send the e-mail, and you won't send the e-mail even if you accidentally hit the keystroke combination for "send."

* Takeaway	Approach people with communication styles comfortable for them.

4-10. RELATIONSHIPS

A Thought on Marriage: "Communication and Common Interests"

Meet Sylvia Brockner, *100 years old* as of this writing. When her husband, Bill, died in 2008, they had been married for sixty-eight years. Sylvia says that the reason for their successful marriage was "communication and common interests." She felt she did not have to elaborate.

Great advice is often short and sweet. After all, there are no secrets to life.

Nip It in the Bud

While some relationship problems dissipate on their own, most often they grow unless resolved. Applying the well-known proverb "A stitch in time saves nine" to relationships means if you have a problem with someone, resolve it while it's still small. A small problem has a way of growing much larger. Define clearly, simply, and without placing fault what you think the problem is, and propose solutions. See idea 4-11 on conflict resolution for more suggestions.

"Please" and "Thank You"

The words "please" and "thank you" still go a long way. One reason relationships fail is that one or both people in them start taking things for granted and forget the basics. No one is required to do anything for you; it is a gift if they do. A "please" upon a request and a "thank you" upon completion—or a thoughtful gesture in return—are always appreciated.

| * Takeaway | Resolve relationship problems while they are still small. |

4-11. CONFLICT RESOLUTION

There are potentially *three* sides to every story: what one person perceived, what the other person perceived, and what really happened. If you're involved in a conflict, determine the views of all sides in the conflict. Don't jump to conclusions after hearing only one or some of the points of view.

When embroiled in a conflict, stay focused on what you want as an outcome. Don't let attempts at manipulation or argument distract you from your desired outcome. When addressing problems with anyone, offer solutions. Write up the problem and what you want as an outcome. If you're reasonable about what you want, the solutions you propose will be received better. If you are talking with your boss, present a copy of what you wrote. This helps him or her focus on the issues as you discuss them.

If you're angry at someone, that person controls you. Instead of showing your anger, first write a letter or e-mail *without* the intention of sending it. The act of writing helps diffuse the anger and enables you to think more clearly about the problem and the possible resolutions. Or talk about the problem with a close friend who knows how to listen.

"For every minute you remain angry, you give up 60 seconds of peace of mind."

—*Ralph Waldo Emerson (1803–1882)*

Robert A. Heinlin (1907–1988), a popular science fiction writer in the 1950s and 1960s, has this advice for men: "If you are in an argument with your wife and you see you are right, apologize immediately."

| * Takeaway | Pick your battles. Not every fight is worth fighting. |
| * Take Action! | Think of a conflict you recently had with someone that didn't end well. What will you do differently next time in a similar situation? |

4-12. PUBLIC SPEAKING IN FRONT OF TWO OR TWO HUNDRED PEOPLE

"The human brain starts working the moment you are born and never stops until you stand up to speak in public."

—*George Jessel (1898–1981)*

It's not as scary as you may imagine. Remember that most of the time when you speak in public, your audience doesn't know what you're going to say! So if you skip a sentence or topic, chances are no one will notice. Here are some tips for successful public speaking:

1. Know your audience. What you have to say should be relevant to your two or two hundred listeners. Opening with self-deprecating humor lets your audience know you're human.
2. Present your key points early; back them up afterward.
3. Don't read your talk. Summarize your key points into bullet points to remind you of your content. Review the bullet points often so you can talk more smoothly.
4. Make eye contact. Look at someone for three seconds before moving on to someone else. Looking less often makes it appear you're nervous; more often seems like staring.
5. Have a backup of your talk. If you're using a tool like Microsoft Power-Point^{tm}, store your file on two separate media in case one fails.
6. Practice in front of a mirror. Are you slouching? Don't! Are you shifting from foot to foot? Don't!
7. "Be sincere. Be bold. Be seated." (Franklin Delano Roosevelt, 1882–1945)

The organization Toastmasters International (www.toastmasters.org) is a leader in helping people improve public speaking. There are chapters all over the world and likely one near you. You can check it out as a guest. If you join—there's a nominal charge—you'll have an opportunity soon after to give a talk. You'll receive feedback from everyone on what you did well and what you can improve.

* Takeaway	Public speaking is an acquired skill and not life threatening ☺.

* Take Action!   Volunteer to speak in front of a group. Practice the
                        points described in this section.
                        Check out a Toastmasters session as a guest.

4-13. WHAT ARE YOUR NEWS SOURCES AND WHY?

What are your news sources and why? On what basis do you accept or reject news? Making positive decisions depends on information in which you can rely and act on.

Remember, *everything* you hear is an opinion, but only some opinions are fact. On what basis do you decide issues? Going back to defining your terms, what is a "fact"? How do you decide if something is a fact or a wrong opinion?

News reports sometimes lead with the phrase "experts say." Just who *are* these "experts"? How often have you heard a newscaster name these "experts"? Same thing for stories that include the phrase "studies show." *Whose* studies? Who commissioned them? How were the studies performed? Who paid for them? Were they accurate and honest? Was there a political motivation for the study? Beware of "studies show"!

* Takeaway   Hear all sides of an issue, then think for yourself.
* Take Action!   Find out the source of the study the next time you
                       encounter "studies show."

4-14. ADVERTISING'S IMPACT ON YOUR LIFE

The two simple purposes that advertising serves are to make you aware of

1. New products and services; and
2. How little you have, how inferior you are compared to other people, how you won't be happy until you buy a product, what qualities and "stuff" you lack, what you really "need," and how much more beautiful other people are than you.

For example, though the purpose of a car is to get you from Point A to Point B, cars are advertised as self-esteem boosters. Say, what's that? You have only the thirty-seventh generation of a mobile phone? Then you *need* the thirty-eighth!

* Takeaway   Recognize that some advertising tries to convince you how inferior or deficient you are. Laugh at the ad!

4-15. LOOK PEOPLE IN THE EYE

Look people in the eye when you talk to them. Looking away is said to imply timidity, shyness, or secrecy. Pick one eye to look at during a conversation. This eliminates any rapid back-and-forth movement of your eyes, which is distracting, and shows the person you are focused on him or her.

* Takeaway   Look people in the eye. Pick an eye and focus on that eye.

4-16. NO "DIGITAL TATTOOS"

Though removable with a considerable amount of money and pain, tattoos are essentially permanent. A "digital tattoo" is text or an image that you upload to the internet. Once online, it is *extremely* difficult to remove, just like a tattoo. Find other ways to communicate your "self" on the internet. One guideline is any text or image you would share with your grandmother.

* Takeaway   Avoid digital tattoos. Consider that *anything* you upload to the internet can be used against you.

4-17. CLEAN UP YOUR SOCIAL MEDIA

Because potential employers will check your social media, keep it clean. Remove the photos of wild parties or anything that a potential employer might look at unfavorably. Beware of and be aware of your digital tattoos.

* Takeaway   Keep your social media clean.
* Take Action!   Review *all* of your social media, and clean it up.

4-18. COMMON MISTAKES IN COMMUNICATION

1. Hoping people will know or somehow figure out what you want without articulating what you want.
2. Imposing on others your concepts of the terms you define.

3. Imposing on others your concepts of right and wrong after you answer questions like "How do you know you're right?"

4. Not speaking up enough when you feel someone is not communicating openly and honestly with you. Ignoring your gut feelings.

5. Letting small problems fester until they become bigger and much harder to deal with. There's a saying that says, "What goes away by itself comes back by itself."

6. In marriage or other committed relationships, not spending enough time listening to and responding to your significant other.

7. Talking too much.

"We have two ears and one mouth so that we can listen twice as much as we speak."

—Epictetus (ca. 55–135 CE)

TAKEAWAY SUMMARY

4.1. You *can* get your point across quickly.

4-2. Define clearly for yourself the important words that shape your future.

4-3. Answering "How do I know I am right?" on any subject helps you clarify your thoughts and proceed to your goals.

4-4. All facts are opinions; not all opinions are facts.

4-5. "Whenever you find yourself on the side of the majority, it is time to pause and reflect."

4-5. "Time makes more converts than reason."

4-6. Recognize and separate what are your or others' problems to solve.

4-7. Be careful to use or interpret the correct meaning of words so you don't mislead people or mislead yourself.

4-8. Weigh carefully any advice given by people with no stake in the outcome.

4-9. Approach people with communication styles comfortable for them.

4-10. Resolve relationship problems while they are still small.

4-11. Pick your battles. Not every fight is worth fighting.

4-12. Public speaking is an acquired skill and not life threatening ☺.

4-13. Hear all sides of an issue, then think for yourself.

4-14. Recognize that some advertising tries to convince you how inferior or deficient you are. Laugh at the ad!

4-15. Look people in the eye. Pick one eye and focus on that one eye.

4-16. Avoid digital tattoos.

4-17 Keep your social media clean.

Entering and Adjusting to the Workplace

"Leaders determine if a company is a great place to work."

—Source: *www.thepeoplegroup.com*

The main ideas to consider while entering and adjusting to the workplace are how to do the following:

- Prepare for, conduct, and follow up on an interview.
- Ask for the job.
- Respond if you don't get the job.
- Get great reference letters.
- Get great raises.
- Negotiate for the win-win.
- Protect your most valuable asset in the real world.
- Define your ideal company to work with.
- Get ahead at work.
- Prepare impressive reports and presentations.
- Stop making excuses.
- Apply the 80–20 rule.
- Handle legal matters.
- Consider volunteering.
- Avoid common mistakes in entering and adjusting to the workplace.

5-1. INTERVIEWING

Before an Interview

Before an interview, prepare by getting to know yourself and the company. Here are some ways:

1. Most colleges have career development services that include simulated interviews in which you can practice being interviewed and hearing typical questions. Take notes and review the questions after the interview to develop crisp, clear, and concise answers.

2. Consider the pros and cons of working with a small, medium, or large company. (See idea 7-19 for the Ben Franklin decision tool.) For example, in a small company it is easier to get noticed, while in a large company there are typically more opportunities for advancement.

3. Visit the company's website to learn about its products and services. Search online for information about the company. What is its reputation? What are recent successes and failures? Why? After you answer these questions, do you still want to work with the company?

4. Decide whether what you would do for the company is how you want to spend eight to ten hours a day, five to six days a week. Or consider that this could be a door-opening job at which you might work briefly before advancing to a more appealing job.

5. Know how the company or organization is faring. Is it profitable or not? If it's a nonprofit organization, is it solid or teetering? During the interview, you can use this information to describe how you can benefit the company.

6. Find out about the company's senior management and decide whether they are leaders you want to work with. Google their names. Do their values and the company's values match yours? Is the company headed in a direction that excites you?

7. Prepare a list of specific questions for interviewers. Here are some sample questions:

   a. What are the top two advantages of working with ABC? (Always use the name of the company.) Notice that the question has a specific number and does not simply ask, "What are the top advantages of working here?" This focuses the interviewers' thinking while also giving them the latitude to say more if they wish.

   b. What are the top two ways to grow professionally and personally here?

    c. What are the top two challenges facing the company or organization now?

8. Call or e-mail a day or two before the interview to confirm the date, time, and location. Confirm, too, what you are expected to bring to the interview. Bring additional material that shows off your excellence.

9. Arrive fifteen to twenty minutes before the interview and simply observe the staff. What is the atmosphere like? Pleasant? Tense? Do the people interact with respect or not? Get a sense of the company culture.

    * Takeaway   Prepare for an interview with the approaches described in this section.

Note: The next few sections consist almost entirely of takeaways, so the takeaways are not highlighted.

During an Interview

Keep in mind that interviewers *want* you to succeed and are not your enemy! After all, they want to succeed, too, by hiring the best people. Typically, interviewers will assume they control the meeting, so initially follow their lead.

A common interview question is "Why should we hire *you*?" Interviewees often squirm, hesitate, and say humdrum things like, "I'm a great worker!" Prepare in advance a clear, crisp answer that differentiates you from others. (This also helps you see for yourself what you offer a company.) Counting off on your fingers while citing three or more reasons to hire you is a strong, positive, visual response. Try out your answer on family and friends for feedback. Go one step further: Ask family and friends why they think someone should hire you. You may learn positive things about yourself you didn't know.

Another question frequently asked is "Where do you see yourself in three years?" (Or five or ten or any number of years.) Again, have a crisp, clear answer ready, which means you need to spend time beforehand thinking that through—a healthy exercise. Where *do* you want to be in three or five years?

A third popular interview question is "How would you handle . . ." and you are presented with a hypothetical situation. The purpose of the question is for the interviewers to see how you handle new situations and think on your feet. The following answer is usually well received: "I appreciate the question, but every situation has a history and usually more than one point of view. I like to learn the background and talk with the people involved, then use my best judgment." This response does not commit you to a specific solution that might not be what the interviewers are looking for.

Because the person asking the questions gets more information than the one answering them, take control of the interview by asking your own questions. Here's one way: when asked a question, respond, "I'll be glad to answer your questions, but is it OK if I ask a few questions first?" It's hard for an interviewer to say no. Be sure you eventually do answer the original question or you might be perceived as evasive. You can start your response to where you see yourself in three years by politely asking, "Where does the company see itself in three years?"

Types of Questions to Ask during an Interview

Use open-ended questions rather than closed-ended questions. The former let you hear more what is on the interviewer's mind; the latter typically have yes or no for an answer. Consider these two questions and the amount of information you can get from each of them:

Closed-ended: "Does ABC company have a good work environment?"

Open-ended: "How would you describe ABC's work environment?" (Remember to use the company's name.)

An alternative to the second question is something like "What are the top two aspects of the work environment here?" Questions like this help the person you're asking to focus. Sometimes asking a question with many answers makes it harder for someone to focus on a specific answer. For example, if you ask the interviewer "What are the *five* best aspects of the work environment here?" she might have difficulty prioritizing them and remembering which aspects she has answered.

Other useful questions:

1. What opportunities for advancement are there with ABC? (Use the name of the company.)
2. What is the biggest challenge of working at ABC?
3. Where does ABC want to be in three to five years? (If not already asked.)

After all, you want to find out whether you'll be happy at the company, too!

By the way, if you receive an answer to what the best aspect of the company is, you can always ask what the next best one is, just not at the same time as the first question.

To work in your points you want to hammer home, feel free to rephrase questions and expand on your answers. But always be sure to include the answer to the questions you're asked. For example, say you are asked, "What is the most valuable trait you offer a company?" You can respond with something like, "There are several traits I offer ABC. I excel at finding several approaches to solving problems and working with different personalities, but I believe that adapting to change is my strongest point."

Always use words that you are comfortable with, not necessarily the answers and phrases used here.

Closing an Interview with Power and Conviction

Toward the end of an interview, you might be asked, "Do you have any other questions?" The following powerful closing question for sales presentations also works well for interviews: "Are you concerned about anything we discussed? Is there anything I haven't answered to your satisfaction? If so, I'd like to address it."

This shows that you accept criticism and deal with problems openly. More importantly, it gives you the opportunity to resolve any issues the interviewer has with you. Rarely are there no concerns. We're all human, and we're bound not to see eye to eye at a first meeting.

By the way, this type of question works well in personal relationships, too. ☺

Ask for the Job!

Yes, ask for the job! Interviews often end with the interviewer saying, "Well, thank you for coming in." The interviewee typically responds, "Thank you, too. Have a nice day." Lame!

As the saying goes: "One hundred percent of what you don't ask for you don't get." (And be prepared to hear no. A lot. ☺)

So ask for the job! Let them know why the company will be better off with you there! Words like these go a long way: "Thank you for your time and perspectives. I like what I researched beforehand and heard today, and I want the job. I'm available to start on . . ." Ask, too, when the company is planning to make its decision. (Your urgency is not their urgency, so be patient.) Then tell them you'll follow up at that time, giving you an opening to contact them again. You might also detect their level of interest by seeing how enthusiastically they respond to your offer to contact them. Still, don't read too much into their reaction as you really don't know each other.

After an Interview

Using your own or store-bought thank-you cards, handwrite a two- to four-sentence thank-you note right after the interview. Handwrite the envelope, mark it "Personal," and mail it on the same day if you can. Handwritten means personal attention, something you want to give when you are beginning a business relationship. Not many people get handwritten notes. Marking the envelope "Personal" increases the chances of your note being opened and read.

In the thank-you note, incorporating a topic discussed during the interview reminds the interviewers of you and shows the note is not a form letter. The interviewers see many people a day, so refresh their memories and reinforce what you know is unique about you. Close with something like, "I'll contact you next Thursday to check on my application." This gives you an excuse to call them and might affect whether they take your call or not. Follow through with a call on the day you say you will.

If you don't trust your spelling, type the note on the computer and use the spell-checker. Then write it out.

The handwritten note serves a few purposes:

1. Few people receive such notes anymore. They stand out, get opened, and get read.
2. You're showing respect for the recipient's time by keeping it short.
3. They will probably not read a full-page letter because of lack of time.

If you have poor handwriting even in block letters, then get thank-you cards that you can print from a computer. Be sure to sign your name.

The thank-you note sets the stage for you to call. If you call and don't get through, call back a few days later to indicate your interest. Use your judgment as to how often to call so you don't nag.

If You Don't Get the Job

If you're turned down for a job, call (don't e-mail!) to find out why. Some companies won't answer that question because of the litigious world we live in now. Write (don't e-mail!) a handwritten note, thanking the interviewers for considering you and wishing them success with the candidate they selected. A few months after the decision, call again to find out how things are going. Maybe the candidate they hired didn't work out and the door is open again. Maybe there's a new opportunity at the company that fits you even better than the first job you interviewed for.

Note: Some people claim this approach applies to dating, too. ☺

Be aware that you may never know the true reason you didn't get the job. It's the "brother-in-law factor": someone simply hired his or her brother-in-law but was required to go through the motions of interviewing candidates.

5-2. GETTING GREAT REFERENCE LETTERS

How can you get great reference letters? Why, by simply writing them yourself, of course! And yes, there's a catch.

If you have a good enough relationship with people to ask for reference letters, you can get what you want and save them time as well. Ask if you can write the recommendation letter for their approval, and schedule an appointment of ten to fifteen minutes for a few days later. Bring the letter and two electronic copies so the referrer can edit the letter if needed. If you are reasonable, the referrer will sign the letter as is or even add comments you might not have thought of. That's why you bring the electronic copy. Offer to leave one copy of the letter on a flash drive with the referrer whether or not he or she edits the letter. You are giving something in return for your referrer's time and letter.

One of the challenges with this approach is to write so that not all letters sound the same!

Over time, you will accumulate a set of letters that highlights the unique aspects of the services you offer. The letters strengthen your own messages to prospective employers.

5-3. SIDEBAR: WHEN ASKING FOR FAVORS

In general, when asking people for favors like reference letters, keep these
things in mind:

1. Include a way for them to gracefully bow out if they don't want to accommodate your request. For example, when asking for a reference letter (in
   person or by e-mail), you might add, "If you're too busy or don't want to
   provide a reference letter, that's fine, and thanks for the consideration."
2. When arranging a meeting, always let a person know how much time you
   want to meet for and stick to it. If you approach the allotted time, bring up
   that you're almost out of time and don't want to overstay your welcome.
   People generally appreciate your respect for their time and often extend
   the meeting past your original estimate. But remember, your want is not
   necessarily their want.
3. Offer a reasonable deadline so your request is not left open-ended and
   therefore possibly not completed. That's why you ask for a meeting to
   review the letter a few days later.

5-4. GETTING GREAT RAISES

The annual or semiannual review to determine the amount of your raise
doesn't have to be a surprise. Ask your boss to discuss the specific goals for
the next year that have to be attained for you to get the full raise, and put
those goals in writing that you both sign. Discuss, too, the opportunities for
bonuses and put them in writing. Meet with your boss at appropriate inter-
vals throughout the year to see whether goal attainment is on schedule. If
not, make adjustments to your work strategies. The annual review, therefore,
becomes almost an afterthought.

You can apply these ideas even if you are partly through the review cycle.
Ask for a minireview of ten to fifteen minutes to define goals for the remain-
der of the cycle. Have your goals in writing.

Caveat: because of uncertain economic times or poor business performance, your company might not have the funds for the raise when the time
comes. This is a reality in the business world. If the company persists in not
giving the full raise to you or others (for any reason), maybe it's time to consider another company.

5-5. NEGOTIATING FOR THE WIN-WIN

Negotiate so that both sides feel they've won. That's called win-win negotiation. There are terabytes of books, papers, and videos about how to negotiate. Keep in mind these key points:

1. Try to get the other side to present its position first; maybe they will offer what you already want.
2. Be reasonable and look for a win-win. Listen carefully to what the other side is requesting and understand what outcomes they want. No one wants to feel that they lost something in a negotiation by being ignored.
3. Give up something so the other side feels you are truly negotiating. That means deciding in advance what you're willing to give up.
4. If you help people get what they want, they will want to negotiate again with you. Treating a negotiation as the first of many transactions sets a positive tone.
5. After presenting your case, don't talk (or blink). Usually the first one to speak is the one who gives up something or agrees to the proposed terms.
6. Be prepared to walk! If you're negotiating for a car, you don't *need* to buy it at that moment.

Here's one application of the ideas in items 2, 4, 5, and 6. Say you want to buy a mobile phone. Research the phones, accessories (case, car charger, and ear buds), prices, and post-sale support in a few retail stores. Decide on the store you want to buy from and total the prices. Ask for the manager and tell him politely, "I'm ready to buy now. I want to buy a certain phone, case, car charger, and ear buds, and I want to pay a total of $X, tax included." Make X $40 or $50 below the total retail price, tax included. Wait, be quiet, and don't blink. The manager may ask if any sales associate offered you the deal. Answer politely, "No, this is how much I want to pay." In many cases, you save yourself $40 or $50!

Watching the TV show *Pawn Stars* is a fun and educational way to learn negotiating tactics used every day by many businesses and people. (Some episodes are on YouTube.) The show is taped at Gold & Silver Pawn Shop in Las Vegas, Nevada. People bring a wide and wild variety of stuff to pawn. The program shows the owners and sellers negotiating, so you can pick up a few pointers.

Most of the negotiations on *Pawn Stars* are straightforward, but here's an example of a different tactic that one of the owners uses, a variation on "splitting the difference."

OWNER: "How much do you want for it?" (Notice he wants the seller to establish the negotiating range.)

SELLER: "Oh, I was thinking $500 to $600." (If you give a range, the owner will naturally assume the lower number is your starting point.)

OWNER: "This stuff is going to sit on my shelf for a while." (This is not the seller's problem!) "How about $300?"

SELLER: "That's less than I'd like. How about we split the difference at $400 and we have a deal?" (The seller extends his hand.)

OWNER: "How about $250?" (He's *lowering* his bid! This is a scare tactic to make the seller think the $300 offer might be gone.)

SELLER: "I'll take the $300. Thanks!"

And the seller probably feels grateful to get the $300.

Another example of a different negotiation is inviting an expert to assess the seller's item.

OWNER: "How much do you want for it?" (He already knows he wants an expert to evaluate the item, but he wants to establish the seller's range first.)

SELLER: "I'd like $3,000 for it."

OWNER (raising an eyebrow in surprise regardless of the amount the seller gives): "Listen, I don't know much about vintage jukeboxes, so I'd like to invite an expert to evaluate it. Is that okay?"

SELLER: "Sure."

The expert comes and says the item is worth $4,000 to $5,000.

SELLER: "That's great! I want to get the $3,000."

OWNER: "The jukebox is going to sit in my store for a while." (Not the seller's problem!) "I can give you $1,000 for it."

The negotiation eventually ends with the seller getting less than $3,000.

* Takeaway   Always look for a win-win when negotiating.
* Take Action!   Think of the last time a negotiation didn't turn out in your favor and determine whether you looked for a win-win or a win-lose.

5-6. PROTECT YOUR MOST VALUABLE ASSET IN THE REAL WORLD

Regardless of how and when you enter the real world, your reputation is your most valuable asset. Guard it fiercely. You may be the smartest, sharpest, most productive person in the world, but that isn't worth much if you're not dependable. Each time you communicate honestly, you build your reputation. Each time you hype or exaggerate, your reputation plummets.

"Character is much easier kept than recovered."

—Thomas Paine (1737–1809)

"Underpromise; overdeliver."

—Tom Peters (b. 1942), author of a classic book, In Search of Excellence

---

Note: The next few sections contain ideas that are all takeaways, so the takeaways are not highlighted.

5-7. DEFINE YOUR IDEAL COMPANY

What Kind of Company Do You Want to Work With?

What kind of company do you want to work *with*? (Not *for*.) Research the reputations of companies and organizations. Define what kind of environment you want:

1. Established or start-up company?
2. Known for positive treatment of staff
3. Team or individually oriented?
4. Offers opportunities for advancement
5. For-profit, nonprofit, or government?
6. (Add your own criteria)

Find the latest great companies to work with by googling "top companies to work for" or "best companies to work for" in your city or in regions where you'd consider living. *Forbes Magazine* (www.forbes.com) publishes an annual list of the best companies to work for.

What Kind of Leadership Do You Want?

What kind of company or organization leaders do you want to work with? It helps to know the type of leadership a company has and what that leadership means. According to www.BusinessDictionary.com, "Leadership involves

1. establishing a clear vision;
2. sharing that vision with others so that they will follow willingly;
3. providing the information, knowledge, and methods to realize that vision; and
4. coordinating and balancing the conflicting interests of all members and stakeholders."

If you're interested in a company, check out its website and see what its leaders stand for. Does the message on the website match the company's reputation? How do you know what is correct? Check out company reviews. Are the sources reliable? Consistent? Recognize that some negative reviews are published by disgruntled employees.

Understand a Company's or Organization's Culture and Traditions

Companies and organizations have traditions of doing business that are unique to them. There certainly are overlaps from one place to another, but take time to understand what makes a company tick. This will help you and your co-workers get comfortable with each other. One common mistake is to arrive at a company and on day one start trying to change the company culture without knowing what approaches have or have not been successful in the past.

Traditions help the company maintain a persistent public image. Sometimes, though, it's helpful to understand where traditions came from to examine whether they are candidates for change. Here is a quick story about that:

John and Jane are preparing dinner. John is startled to see Jane cut off the ends of the pot roast and throw them out.

John: "Why did you throw away that perfectly good meat?"

Jane: "Why, that's how my mother prepares pot roast."

Curious, John phones his mother-in-law and tells her what her daughter has just done.

John: "Why do *you* cut off the ends of the meat and throw them out?"

Mom: "Why, that's how *my* mother prepares pot roast."

Undeterred, John calls up his grandmother-in-law and tells her how her daughter and granddaughter prepare pot roast.

John: "Your daughter and granddaughter cut off the ends of the pot roast and throw them out. The trail led to you. PLEASE tell me, why do *you* cut off the ends of the meat and throw them out?"

Grandma: "The pot was too small."

While some traditions have sensible roots, the origins of others are obscure or may not be relevant anymore.

The Intellectual Property Agreement

Most companies require as a condition of employment that you sign an intellectual property agreement that says essentially that *anything* you discover or invent while employed with them belongs to them. This often includes discoveries or inventions that are not related to the company's products or services and outside of company time! Some clauses even state that you must help the company apply for patents based on your ideas. If you are working on an idea before you start with a company, negotiate to exclude your idea from a blanket intellectual property agreement.

* Takeaway	"Tradition! How did that tradition get started? I'll tell you. I don't know. But it's a tradition!"
	—*Tevye in* Fiddler on the Roof

5-8. HOW TO GET AHEAD AT WORK

Here are some ideas on how to get ahead at work:

1. Save people time and you'll be a hero. Find ways to help people work more effectively and happily. As we'll see in idea 8-1, time is the only unrecoverable resource.

2. Help others succeed by helping them look good. If you're part of a team, acknowledge the team's role in your success. If you're working alone, acknowledge that the work you're doing relates to others' work. You may hear about people taking credit for others' work, but you'll quickly figure out for yourself who is a team player and who is an intellectual property thief.

3. Mind your own business. Don't be concerned with what others are earning or the cars they drive. Compete with yourself to improve the products or services you provide. If someone else is leading a life you think you would like, ask how the person attained that life. But as the saying goes, "Be careful what you ask for; you might get it."

4. Maintain a positive attitude. It's easy to criticize what does not work well, so always look for ways to improve situations and put forward your own suggestions.

5. Honor deadlines. This goes for small things like returning books on time to big things like completing your part of the company's big project. Learn to politely say no or renegotiate if you feel you are being asked to support an unrealistic or unpleasant commitment.

6. Lose the excuses. Excuses don't run a business; results do.

* Takeaway

"You think I have problems? I just have multiple sclerosis. . . . Some people can't balance a checkbook!"

—Jimmie Heuga (1943–2010), an Olympic medalist skier whose career was shortened by multiple sclerosis

5-9. HOW TO PREPARE IMPRESSIVE REPORTS AND PRESENTATIONS

The reports and presentations you prepare give you opportunities to shine. Here are some techniques:

1. Make your points using as few words as possible. As *The Elements of Style* puts it, "Vigorous writing is concise."

2. Read Milo O. Frank's book *How to Get Your Point Across in 30 Seconds or Less.* It's a short book. ☺

3. Use the "so what?" approach when preparing material: imagine a recipient of your report or presentation will ask "so what?" on *every point* you make. This helps you decide how to word your thoughts or whether to include a point at all.

4. Give the important ideas first and back up every summary idea with relevant details. You save people time, plus you still get your points across if a meeting or presentation ends sooner than planned.

5. Use plenty of white space on the written or displayed page so people can absorb the ideas more easily.

6. Read your report or presentation out loud to yourself. This helps refine your word choices, expose awkward or unclear wording, and find spelling mistakes not caught by a spell-checker. (Example: "Eye sea your hear" is "I see you're here.")

7. "Be sincere; be brief; be seated." This was the advice that Franklin Delano Roosevelt (1882–1945) gave to his son James on public speaking.

8. Include no more than seven lines of text on a single presentation slide.

* Takeaway	Keep reports and presentations simple.
* Take Action!	Practice shortening sentences into concise form without loss of meaning. For example, "four score and seven years ago" becomes "eighty-seven years ago." On a PowerPoint presentation, that reads: ■ 87 years ago leaving room for more words on the same line.

5-10. LOSE THE EXCUSES!

"Trust takes years to build, seconds to lose."

—Anonymous

You build up trust from others by following through on your word and delivering the results you promised, not by falling back on excuses. But sometimes, unexpected events pop up that can derail even the best intentions.

Say your car breaks down on the way to an interview. Rather than calling to cancel or delay the meeting, take a taxi and deal with the car later. Don't even mention that the car broke down. An interviewer might think you don't have reliable transportation, setting a negative tone for the interview. Keep your troubles to yourself; interviewers have their own problems. ☺

Excuses weaken your position. Sure, emergencies arise and most people are understanding and sympathetic when they occur, but decide carefully what are true emergencies.

* Takeaway

> "Ninety-nine percent of the failures come from people who have the habit of making excuses."
>
> —*George Washington Carver (ca. 1864–1943)*

> "He that is good for making excuses is seldom good for anything else."
>
> —*Benjamin Franklin (1706–1790)*

> "I do not buy a service; I buy a *result*."
>
> —*Montoya in* Miami Vice *(2006)*

* Take Action!

Think of a time you gave an excuse for not following through. How would you treat the situation differently now?

5-11. ADVANCE ONE JOB OR POSITION AT A TIME

You'll almost certainly have more than one job and possibly more than one career. Start out with what might be less than the ideal job or position if it allows you to get your foot in the door and gain some experience. Use that experience to look for the job or position that is the next rung up.

5-12. PEOPLE SKILLS VS. TECHNICAL SKILLS: WHICH IS HARDER TO DEVELOP?

People skills and technical skills can both be learned, but people skills are harder to develop. Resources like Nightingale-Conant (www.nightingale .com), Brian Tracy (www.BrianTracy.com), and Denis Waitley (www.waitley .com) offer straightforward, specific tools to help you recognize what people skills you may lack and start making the necessary changes to acquire them.

These people skills are often lacking when you first enter the real world:

1. Listening to what people want
2. Not interrupting when you think you have a better idea
3. Recognizing the importance of teamwork
4. Expressing confidently what you want without threatening other people
5. Answering questions without putting people down

One approach to enhancing people skills is to put yourself in uncomfortable situations and talk or act through the discomfort. If you stay in your comfort zone, you'll never build skills outside of it.

5-13. ACCOUNTABILITY

Wikipedia defines accountability as "the acknowledgment and assumption of responsibility for actions, products, decisions, and policies."

Be accountable to yourself and don't blame others or circumstances if things don't work out as hoped.

This headline appeared on the internet in fall 2013:

ATM ACCIDENTALLY SWAPS FIFTIES FOR TWENTIES

But the ATM didn't do it! A *person* put fifties in an ATM that is supposed to dispense twenties.

How is accountability handled in the private sector? In government? Is there a difference? Why?

Here's an example that raises valid questions regardless of your political views. The Affordable Care Act (Obamacare) website, healthcare.gov, was released on October 1, 2013, and did not work as planned. Who was accountable? In congressional hearings, the secretary of health and human services, Kathleen Sebelius, said she was responsible and accountable.

What did that mean in practice? Did she repay the cost of the fixes to the website? Did her staff? Did she or any of her staff lose their jobs? Does President Obama share responsibility and accountability? Why or why not? What happens when a failure like that occurs in the private sector, such as the credit card data breach at Capital One in 2018? Often, the head of information technology steps down or is fired.

5-14. RESPONSIBILITY AND AUTHORITY

A tricky situation in the workplace is being given responsibility for a project or task without the authority to get the work done. To the extent possible, get the authority, too. If someone else has the authority over your project or task, you might find yourself in a situation where you cannot proceed with your work. Unfortunately, this is a situation that often cannot be avoided, but be aware of the possible conflicts that can emerge.

5-15. THE 80–20 RULE

The 80–20 rule, also called the Pareto principle, is a common and useful rule in business. The rule says 80 percent of the effects come from 20 percent of the causes. One example is that 80 percent of a company's sales often are derived from 20 percent of its customers. Another example common in software development is that 80 percent of the system is developed with the first 20 percent of the effort. (It's always that last 5 percent in software development that takes so much time because software is never done; it always evolves!)

5-16. LEGAL MATTERS

A few suggestions on legal matters:

1. Always read a contract in its entirety before you sign it! *Always!*
2. Speak up if you find clauses you don't agree with. For example, a common clause in employment contracts is the "at will" arrangement. It basically states that a company can fire you or ask you to leave for any reason, with or without justification. This section has worked its way into Corporate America because of the many wrongful termination lawsuits in recent decades.
3. Use the website www.nolo.com as a resource for low-cost legal matters like boilerplate agreements.

5-17. VOLUNTEERING

Is volunteering for you? If so, find an organization that is important to you and volunteer two, four, ten, or however many hours a week or month. Volunteering also enhances a resume. As you get busier building a family, career, and life, substituting monetary donations may lessen the demands on your time.

5-18. COMMON MISTAKES WHEN ENTERING AND ADJUSTING TO THE WORKPLACE

Common mistakes consist of the following:

1. Not learning interviewing skills while still in school.
2. Failing to ask for the job during interviews.
3. Skipping the creation of a portfolio of school accomplishments to show during interviews.
4. Not taking the time to ask yourself, "What kind of company do I want to work with?"
5. Not knowing enough people skills to know that you need to develop people skills.
6. Not negotiating a win-win.

TAKEAWAY SUMMARY

Note: Because most of the chapter consists of takeaways, only the numbered takeaways are summarized here.

5-1. Prepare for an interview with the approaches described in this section.

5-5. Always look for a win-win when negotiating.

5-7. "Tradition! How did that tradition get started? I'll tell you. I don't know. But it's a tradition!"

5-8. "You think I have problems? I just have multiple sclerosis. . . . Some people can't balance a checkbook!"

5-9. Keep reports and presentations simple.

5-10. "Ninety-nine percent of the failures come from people who have the habit of making excuses."

5-10. "He that is good for making excuses is seldom good for anything else."

5-10. "I do not buy a service; I buy a *result*."

6

Life's Situations with Challenging Personalities

The main ideas to consider while learning about life's situations and curious personalities are how to do the following:

- Work alongside different personalities.
- Deal with gruff and generally unpleasant people.
- Deal with complaining coworkers.
- Deal with someone who wants to steal software or any company asset.
- Deal with someone who follows a different religion from you.
- Deal with someone who has a mental illness.
- Deal with other personalities.
- Understand what happens if you lose someone close to you.
- Look for a win-win when dealing with people.
- Avoid common mistakes in handling life's situations and curious personalities.

6-1. WORKING ALONGSIDE DIFFERENT PERSONALITIES

Most people you will encounter in the real world are pleasant to work with. They want to do their best, help others succeed, and work as a team. But you will meet people who are unpleasant, angry, hateful, arrogant, lazy, incompetent, and, well, fill in your favorite list of unsavory qualities. Learning to deal with unpleasant personalities is an acquired skill that is rarely taught in school.

The following sections are scenarios involving such characters. There is no attempt to psychoanalyze *why* they behave that way, only techniques on how to deal with them. The key is to deflect or disarm their behavior without getting sucked into it. It is certainly possible that they are not aware they come across as they do. They have their own life stories and might think their behavior is perfectly normal.

6-2. MEET A GRUFF AND GENERALLY UNPLEASANT PERSON

Here are some behaviors of gruff and generally unpleasant people and how such people might demonstrate the behaviors during a business meeting:

1. Rude—frequently interrupts your talking
2. Tactless—proposes ideas or makes statements that offend you
3. Inconsiderate—keeps you waiting unnecessarily; takes calls while you are meeting
4. Denigrating—puts you or others down with untrue statements

Stay pleasant and focused on your objectives by simply ignoring the negative comments. He or she is trying to get a rise out of you, so ignoring sends a message that you are not getting sucked in. If the problem persists, have a private conversation in which you state that you do not want to be treated that way. Another option is to challenge a distasteful statement by asking what was meant by it or if there is a hidden message. People often back down when "caught."

* Takeaway	Expect *any* behavior and get to know your own.
* Take Action!	Recall two instances when you were unhappy with how you reacted when someone treated you unpleasantly. List three better ways to respond to each

situation the next time it happens. One example is to simply ignore it.

6-3. MEETING AN UNHAPPY, COMPLAINING COWORKER

If a coworker constantly complains to you about his situation at work, offering solutions can be a double-edged sword. On the one hand, you may want to help by offering suggestions, but on the other hand, *you* might have a stake in the outcome, and the advice you offer might place your position in jeopardy.

One response to constant complaining is to suggest that your coworker speak with the people involved and resolve the problems directly with them rather than involving you. If you put up with the complaining, you're sending a message that it's OK to complain to you.

* Takeaway	1. Tell complainers politely to resolve their complaints directly with the people involved.
	2. Don't let things fester; resolve problems while they are small. It will save a lot of people a lot of anguish, including you.
* Take Action!	Think of two times that you were unhappy with your response or reaction to an unpleasant or frustrating situation at work, at school, or in everyday life. List three ways you can respond in the future (or now!) that will lead to a better outcome for you.

6-4. MEETING SOMEONE WHO WANTS TO STEAL SOFTWARE OR OTHER COMPANY ASSETS

All commercially available software is copyrighted; it is illegal to use pirated versions. If you are offered illegal software, a simple "No, thank you" will suffice. However, this can be a sticky situation. If the company policy is not to use illegal software, reminding the offender could create tension between you two—especially if the offender is your boss. Consider informing the appropriate department (usually human resources) anonymously (if that is at all possible in today's world).

* Takeaway   Stay away from illegal software.
* Take Action!   Write two times when you allowed your principles
                    to be challenged and did not respond in a way that
                    satisfied you. Write three ways you will respond
                    differently in the future for a healthier outcome.

6-5. MEETING SOMEONE WHO FOLLOWS A DIFFERENT RELIGION

In the workplace as in life, accept that there will be people of many different
religions. Everyone has a story.

* Takeaway

"Congress shall make no law respecting an establishment of religion, or prohibiting the free exercise thereof; or abridging the freedom of speech,
or of the press; or the right of the people peaceably
to assemble, and to petition the Government for a
redress of grievances."

—*US Constitution, First Amendment (ratified 1791)*

6-6. MEETING SOMEONE WITH A MENTAL ILLNESS

Mental illness is discussed and dealt with much more openly now than just a
few decades ago. One in four Americans (that's 25 percent of the population)
is affected by mental illness directly or indirectly. That means one in four
Americans has a mental illness, knows friends or relatives who have one, or
works alongside someone (or many people) who have one.

Some individuals feel discomfort or fear around people in wheelchairs or
with cancer. Some also feel discomfort or fear around people with mental
illnesses. They wonder, "When will the 'patient' erupt again? Is he or she vio-
lent? What can I do or say to help? Or should I just turn away and not deal
with it?" Understanding mental illnesses helps overcome this discomfort and
helps in working with or knowing mentally ill people.

If you suspect mental illness in yourself or others, get help *now*! Many colleges have resources—often at no additional cost—for dealing with mental
illness. Check at yours. The reference section has several other resources.

* Takeaway	At some point in your life, you will probably encounter someone with a mental illness.
* Take Action!	If you think you or someone you know has a mental illness, deal with it *now* before it gets worse and begins to have a negative effect on your life and the lives of those close to you.

6-7. WHAT INDICATES A MENTAL ILLNESS?

It is challenging for laypeople to detect symptoms of a mental illness. Such illnesses are woven into the personality, unlike other genetic illnesses such as diabetes. Be aware that mental illness is a *pattern*, a series of similar behaviors, not just one or two unusual events. Expressions like "Oh, I'm so bipolar today!" or "That is so OCD!" (obsessive-compulsive disorder) describe an event, not a pattern.

The first flags indicating a possible mental illness are behavior that is out of character and poor judgment that causes emotional or physical harm to the person, loved ones, friends, or, for that matter, anyone. Most people tend to behave the same way, or "in character," most of the time. But people also have "bad days" and "out of character" days, so one "wild hour" or "wild day" does not necessarily mean the individual has a mental illness. When behavior changes radically and irrationally over time, however, a mental illness might be the root cause.

* Takeaway	"Be kind, for everyone you meet is fighting a hard battle." —*Ian Maclaren (1850–1907)*
	"At some point in your life, you will probably encounter someone with a mental illness." —*Ian Maclaren (1850–1907)*
* Take Action!	Learn about the more common symptoms of the common (yes, common) mental illnesses like bipolar disorder, obsessive-compulsive disorder, and schizophrenia.

6-8. MEETING MANY OTHER PERSONALITIES

In the workplace and in life, you will meet other people from different cultures, genders, races, ages, generations, and religions. You will also meet people with mental and physical disabilities. Try viewing people as part of a one-level hierarchy of humanity that does not have classifications or categories. Each person has a story that caused him or her to develop a certain way. If you understand that story, you can understand what motivates that person and how you can help that person attain his or her goals while still pursuing yours.

* Takeaway	Treat each person as an individual, not as a member of some category.
* Take Action!	List two times when you withdrew from a situation because someone was behaving "weirdly." Write three ways you will respond or react differently the next time that happens.

6-9. IF SOMEONE CLOSE TO YOU DIES OR LEAVES

Dr. Elisabeth Kübler-Ross's classic book, *On Death and Dying*, includes a detailed discussion of the five stages of grief when someone close to you has a terminal illness or leaves you. (Some of the quotations come from the Wikipedia page for "Kübler-Ross model.") The five stages are as follows:

1. Denial	"I feel fine"; "This can't be happening, not to me"; "I can't believe he's sick."
2. Anger	"Why me? It's not fair!"; "How can this happen to me?"; "Who is to blame?"
3. Bargaining	"I'll do anything for a few more years"; "I will give my life savings if . . ."
4. Depression	"I'm so sad, why bother with anything?"; "I am (or my loved one is) going to die soon, so what's the point?"; "I miss my loved one, why go on?"
5. Acceptance	"It's going to be okay"; "I can't fight it; I may as well prepare for it"; "I accept that his dying wasn't my

fault"; "We did all we could do to help her last days be peaceful."

Dr. Kübler-Ross's book also has a powerful message on the loss of a loved one or a relationship: the opposite of love is not hate, but indifference. A common reaction when someone no longer loves you is a feeling of anger or hate. When you eventually become indifferent to that person, you are over it. Dr. Kübler-Ross discusses in detail how to do that.

* Takeaway	Acknowledging grief is the first step to deal with it.
* Take Action!	Read *On Death and Dying*.

6-10. LOOK FOR A WIN-WIN
In every transaction or interaction with people, look for a win-win for both sides. If you get what you want while helping the other side get what they want, you are building a positive, healthy relationship. Stay away from and don't create win-lose or lose-lose situations.

* Takeaway	Win-win interactions set the stage for more win-win interactions.
* Take Action!	Whether you won or lost, write two times when you were party to a win-lose transaction. Write three ways you can turn a similar situation into a win-win next time.

6-11. COMMON MISTAKES IN LIFE'S SITUATIONS WITH CHALLENGING PERSONALITIES
This is actually a topic for an entire other book! But here are some major ones:

1. Denying the possibility that you or someone you know has a mental illness.
2. Getting sucked into winless arguments.
3. Not honoring the First Amendment's commitment to freedom of religion.
4. Not defining how you want to be treated.
5. Making win-lose transactions instead of win-win transactions.

TAKEAWAY SUMMARY

6-2. Expect *any* behavior and get to know your own.

6-3. Tell complainers politely to resolve their complaints directly with the people involved.

6-3. Don't let things fester; resolve problems while they are small. It will save a lot of people a lot of anguish, including you.

6-4 Stay away from illegal software.

6-5. "Congress shall make no law respecting an establishment of religion, or prohibiting the free exercise thereof; or abridging the freedom of speech, or of the press; or the right of the people peaceably to assemble, and to petition the Government for a redress of grievances."

6-7. At some point in your life, you will encounter someone with a mental illness.

6-7. "Be kind, for everyone you meet is fighting a hard battle."

6-8. Treat each person as an individual, not as a member of some category.

6-9. Acknowledging grief is the first step to deal with it.

6-10. Win-win interactions set the stage for more win-win interactions.

7

Personal Improvement

"Courage is resistance to fear, mastery of fear, not absence of fear."

—Mark Twain (1835–1910)

The main ideas to consider while improving yourself personally and professionally are how to do the following:

- Build self-esteem.
- Use positive self-talk.
- Develop a positive growth mind-set.
- Determine your strengths and weaknesses.
- Set goals.
- Manage time, projects, and tasks.
- Deal with "the stress of life."
- Learn how to fulfill your potential.
- Discern good and bad judgment.
- Recognize what is possible, impossible, or just hard.
- Guarantee your work.
- Handle ignorance and awareness.
- Avoid the use of common phrases that hold you back.
- Learn to use the Ben Franklin decision tool.
- Avoid common mistakes when working on improving yourself personally.

7-1. A PERSPECTIVE ON PERSONAL IMPROVEMENT

"The only constant in nature is change."

—Heraclitus (ca. 535–475 BCE), Greek philosopher

What does "personal improvement" mean? How about just the word "improvement"—what does that mean? Who decides when you have "improved"? How can *you* tell if you have improved?

That's up to you to decide for yourself. Some ways to tell that you have improved are if you:

1. Feel happier than you did before
2. Handle an unpleasant situation better than in the past
3. Attain goals more easily and more frequently
4. Develop deeper, more meaningful relationships with family, friends, or a significant other

When you take responsibility for your actions to create the life you want, you are helping yourself change in a healthy direction.

"If you don't make the time to work on creating the life you want, you're eventually going to be forced to spend a LOT of time dealing with a life you don't want."

—Kevin Ngo (b. 1978)

"It takes a lot of energy to hold back reality."

—C. Norman Coleman (b. 1945)

* Takeaway

"When you're finished changing, you're finished."

—Benjamin Franklin (1706–1790)

* Take Action!

List five things that represent "personal improvement" to you. Pick one and start working on it!

(See the references for some sources of personal improvement material.)

7-2. BUILDING SELF-ESTEEM

"If someone talked to you like you talked to yourself, you'd punch them in the face."

—Anonymous

If you like yourself, skip to the next section. If not, here's one way to start. Write "I like myself!" in big bold letters on an index card. Read it aloud—with passion—again and again several times a day. It's hard not to smile and feel better! (This suggestion comes from material available at www.waitley.com.) This is the "Big Truth" approach: repeat something often enough and you start believing it. Caution—some advertisers use the "Big Lie" approach: hear something often enough and you start believing it!

Now write "I like myself!" at the top of a piece of paper and list at least twenty-eight reasons *why* you like yourself. You'll be amazed at what you didn't consciously know about yourself.

Take more action! From that list, write on an index card or in your mobile device two things you will do differently starting now to bring out two of the twenty-eight positive qualities you wrote down. Read the message aloud and with strong, passionate emotions four or five times a day. For example, you might write "I am *always* on time!" to reinforce that you respect people's time.

When you believe without hesitation what you are saying, move on to the next set of two of your twenty-eight positive qualities. Soon you'll discover a lot more than twenty-eight positive qualities. These first-person statements are called *affirmations* and are discussed again in the next section.

Possession of material things is not a measure of self-esteem, though it might measure a sense of accomplishment. For example, the car you drive is intended to take you from one place to another, not to boost your self-esteem. ☺

One way to build self-esteem is to always do your best. That way you can't fault yourself if things don't work out as planned or hoped. Professional golfer Nancy Lopez (b. 1957) put it this way: "Do your best, one shot at a time, and then move on." Doing your best also forces you to compete with yourself to improve and to concern yourself less with what others are accomplishing (and saying about you).

"You can't change the hand you were dealt, but you *can* change the way you play it."

—*C. Norman Coleman (b. 1945)*

| * Takeaway | Practice "I like myself!" at least five times a day. Out loud and with *feeling*! |
| * Take Action! | Practice "I like myself!" at least five times a day. Out loud and with *feeling*! (Repeated for emphasis; this is one step on the path toward self-esteem.) |

7-3. WHAT IS YOUR EMOTIONAL INTELLIGENCE?

Daniel Goleman created the concept of Emotional Intelligence (EI), which he claims can be more important than one's Intelligence Quotient (IQ). Defining EI as how well we handle ourselves in our relationships, he identifies four areas of EI:

1. Self-awareness: How well are you in touch with your emotions?
2. Self-management: How well do you manage your emotions?
3. Empathy: How well do you relate to what others are feeling?
4. Skilled relationships: How skilled are you at handling your relationships?

For a brief overview of EI, view Mr. Goleman's introduction at https://www.youtube.com/watch?v=Y7m9eNoB3NU&app=desktop.

Mr. Goleman also points out that the brain circuitry that supports EI is the last to mature. How mature is yours?

| * Takeaway | Learn what your Emotional Intelligence is. |
| * Take Action! | Read Mr. Goleman's book *Emotional Intelligence: Why It Can Matter More Than IQ* (2005). |

7-4. POSITIVE SELF-TALK; OR, WHAT DO YOU THINK OF YOURSELF?

How you talk to yourself defines how you'll feel about and respond to situations. Baseball players with a .300 batting average are considered very good.

But a .300 batting average means they still will be out 70 percent of the time. A batter probably tells himself, "I'm getting a hit now." It's unlikely the batter is thinking, "I'll probably be out."

Use only positive self-talk like "I'm smart, so I will solve this problem." And not "I'm stupid; I'll never figure this thing out." Learn more about self-talk and positive affirmations from Dr. Denis Waitley and Brian Tracy. (See www.waitley.com, www.BrianTracy.com, and www.nightingale.com.)

Dr. Waitley poses this question in one of his affirmation programs: "What was sixteen-year-old gymnast Mary Lou Retton thinking seconds before launching her final program during the 1984 Olympic Games?" To win the gold medal, she *had* to score a perfect 10. Not a 9.95, but a 10. Was she thinking, "I'll probably screw up!"? Or was she thinking, "I'm gonna nail this perfect 10 just like in practice!"? Self-talk is *critical*! You can see Ms. Retton's final program on YouTube at https://www.youtube.com/watch?v=Sya66z4mCiA. Yes, she scored a perfect 10 and won the gold medal!

Another way to look at this is this: "Always act as if you will succeed" (Anonymous).

To learn healthier self-talk, you can also search the web for "inspirational quotes" or search specifically for the quotes of someone you respect. See www.BrainyQuote.com for quotes by author and by topic.

* Takeaway	Use only positive, constructive self-talk.
* Take Action!	Write three negative things you still say to yourself. Write three positive things you will say to yourself the next time a similar circumstance happens. For example, don't say, "I didn't answer that question well. I'm such an idiot!" Instead, you can say, "I didn't answer that question well; next time I'll . . ." Or simply acknowledge the situation by admitting, "I didn't answer that question well." Don't put yourself down.

7-5. YOUR MIND-SET

Dr. Carol S. Dweck's breakthrough book, *Mindset: the New Psychology of Success*, presents two major concepts: the fixed mind-set and the growth mind-set. People with fixed mind-sets believe they are born with the intelligence they will have their entire lives; intelligence cannot be improved on. They have difficulty accepting failure as it implies low or inadequate intelligence. People with growth mind-sets believe intelligence can be increased with a positive attitude and a positive reaction to failure.

Most of Dr. Dweck's research in education focuses on grades K–12, but the ideas apply just as well to adults and life in general. The fixed and growth mind-sets can be illustrated with these two perspectives, respectively: "I'm not good at math" and "I'm not good at math *yet*."

What is your mind-set? Dr. Dweck points that most people are a mixture of fixed and growth, but you *can* move toward the growth mind-set using tools described in her book. Consider how you react to failure. Do you say you did your best but you just didn't "have it" or analyze why you failed and what you can do differently next time in similar situations?

* Takeaway	You *can* grow your intelligence with a growth mind-set.
* Take Action!	Read *Mindset!* Chapter 2 describes and compares the two mind-sets, and chapter 8 explains how to change mind-sets.

7-6. DETERMINE YOUR STRENGTHS AND WEAKNESSES

What are your strengths and weaknesses?

Your strengths are your qualities that cause you to feel better about yourself, and your weaknesses are your qualities that cause you to feel worse about yourself. To get a handle on both, write a list of your strengths and weaknesses. Pick one of each at a time and learn about them. Think and feel about how the strength arose and how to, well, strengthen it. Examine the weakness you selected to learn what about it causes you to feel worse and what steps you can take to change direction. See www.nightingale.com and search for "convert weaknesses to strengths."

Consider this advice for adding to your strengths:

"Build up your weaknesses until they become your strong points."

—*Knute Rockne (1888–1931)*

| * Takeaway | Work on weaknesses one at a time, converting them to strengths. |
| * Take Action! | Identify two of your weaknesses. (If you have none, please publish how you did it.) Write three steps you'll take to recognize them when they reveal themselves and three steps you'll take to respond or react positively. |

7-7. GOAL SETTING

"If you don't know where you are going, you might end up someplace else."

—*Yogi Berra (1925–2015)*

A goal is simply a desired result. The brain responds to and is motivated by clear, precise goals with deadlines. "Let's go to the mountains sometime" is not a goal. "Let's leave tomorrow at 8:00 a.m. to go snowshoeing in Breckenridge" is a goal.

Write goals that begin with "I *will*," as in "I *will* complete the project by Tuesday at 1:00 p.m." and not "I will not be late on the project." The brain needs clear images of what to do and what to take action on. Writing or saying "I will not" does not give direction to the brain on what to actually *do*.

Another way of looking at this is to imagine how a child is supposed to respond to a parent's request (demand?) to "Clean up!" or "Be good!" What does that mean to the child? The child needs specific instructions on what cleaning up means: "Put the books back on the bookshelf" or "Put your dishes in the sink when you're done." The brain works best with specific instructions.

See www.nightingale.com and www.waitley.com for excellent material on goal setting.

| * Takeaway | Set clear, specific goals with deadlines. |
| * Take Action! | Set two new goals now. Find resources to learn goal-setting techniques that you're comfortable with. If you don't know where to begin, try the resources listed in this section. |

7-8. "THE STRESS OF LIFE"

In his classic book, *The Stress of Life*, published in 1956, Dr. Hans Selye (1907–1982) applied the word "stress" to human activities for the first time. He defines stress as "the non-specific response of the body to any demand for change" (called *stressors*). Note that this includes "*any* demand or change." There is neither "good" nor "bad" in the definition; it's all in how you react to and handle your stress, no matter the source.

How you handle stress affects your health and your responses to stressful situations. The key is to recognize that you can *choose* your reaction to stress (or any other stimulus). In her TED video on making stress your friend, Dr. Kelly McGonigal explains how to harness stress positively. She shows that the heart-pounding reaction to a negative stressor like a safety threat is physiologically the same as the heart-pounding reaction to a positive stressor like a hug. Her TED talk is at www.ted.com/talks/kelly_mcgonigal_how_to_make _stress_your_friend.

* Takeaway	You *can* learn to respond positively to negative stressful situations. As quoted earlier in chapter 3, the stanza from Edmund Vance Cooke's poem "How Did You Die?" is appropriate here, too.

> Oh, a trouble's a ton, or a trouble's an ounce,
> Or a trouble is what you make it,
> And it isn't the fact that you're hurt that counts,
> But only how did you take it?

* Take Action!	1. Watch Dr. McGonigal's video.
	2. Write down two stressors, one positive and one negative. Examine the similarities and differences when you compare your emotional response to each of them.

7-9. "GETTING THINGS DONE"

In his best-selling book *Getting Things Done*, last published in 2015, David Allen (b. 1945) presents a complete system for dealing with tasks or projects, whether ones that take a minute or ones that might take years. Mr. Allen claims, "Your head is for having ideas—not for *holding* them." His system ties in nicely with the previous section on stress. Two of his many ideas in the book follow.

1. If a task takes less than two minutes, *do it now*! It will take longer to make a note to do the task later, recall the note, and hopefully remember what it was you wanted to do. Worse, of course, is forgetting to do the task altogether. This idea has to be taken in context, of course. If your house is on fire, the two-minute task can wait. ☺
2. Use a "Collection Bucket" to hold ideas that need to be addressed later. The bucket is a list and/or a collection of notes that are handwritten or stored in your mobile device. Using a Collection Bucket enables you to stay focused on what you're doing now and not get distracted by other less urgent or less important tasks. You can revisit the Collection Bucket later or during the weekly review that the author recommends.

Note that the 2015 edition was completely rewritten from the original 2001 edition to incorporate using technology like mobile phones and tablets.

* Takeaway	Use the well-established system described in Mr. Allen's book.
* Take Action!	1. Purchase or check out *Getting Things Done* from the library.
	2. Create a Collection Bucket to keep ideas that need to be addressed later. Remember to access the Collection Bucket!

7-10. USE A TO-DO LIST

A to-do list keeps you focused on what is important and urgent and helps you allocate your time. Maintain the list by rewriting and prioritizing it at the end of every day. Rewriting it helps direct your brain to process the items in the subconscious. The brain *does* process thoughts while you sleep, so giving it material to work with helps you develop solutions. Be sure to include in the to-do list some fun things to do after completing the higher-priority items.

Given a choice of equal priorities, do the hard tasks first. When you complete a task, cross it off *emphatically*, giving you a sense of satisfaction and accomplishment. You will probably feel closer to your goals, which also generates feelings of satisfaction and accomplishment.

There are mobile-phone apps for keeping to-do lists; search the App Store or Google Play for "to-do list." As of this writing, there are hundreds of apps to help you organize your to-do list. Or use a "numbered list" feature in a word processor or spreadsheet, which makes it easy to add, remove, and update entries, as well as to reprioritize them. An example that includes some time estimates can be found in figure 7.1.

Sample To-Do List – Preparing for the Next Semester of Teaching (partial list; some time estimates in hours)

General

1. Create reports for prior semester's courses – 2
2.

Course CS 1050

1. Complete the Table of Contents of files to upload to Blackboard
2. Set course dates in the *Course at a Glance* file – 0.5
3. Upload all files to Blackboard – 0.5
   a. TOC
   b. Course at a Glance
   c. Course Policies
   d. Richest Man in Babylon assignment
   e. Assignments
   f. PowerPoints of chapters from the textbook
4. Update homework assignments
5.

Course CS 1400

1. Prepare answer set for selected homework problems
2. Complete the Table of Contents of files to upload
3. Set course dates in the *Course at a Glance* file
4. Upload all files to Blackboard
   a. TOC
   b. Course at a Glance
   c. Course Policies
   d. Richest Man in Babylon assignment
   e. Assignments
5. Update homework assignments

FIGURE 7.1.   To-Do List with Time Estimates

One powerful and flexible PC-based desktop product for setting reminders is Kirby Alarm Pro (Windows desktop) by Ian Cook. You can use it to write to-do lists, sett program reminders, schedule programs to run automatically, and much more. See www.kirbyfooty.com/product-kirbyalarm.php.

* Takeaway	Use a daily to-do list.
* Take Action!	1. Create a to-do list now for today. (And, if it's late in the day, for tomorrow. ☺)
	2. Purchase Kirby Alarm.

7-11. "GOOD" AND "BAD" JUDGMENT

What do "good" judgment and "bad" judgment mean? First, let's note that the Oxford English Dictionary defines judgment as "the ability to make considered decisions or come to sensible conclusions." Conclusions aren't always sensible, however, so we'll define judgment only as "the ability to make considered decisions or come to conclusions."

To develop good judgment, examine and learn from the consequences of bad judgment. In other words, make *new* mistakes now in order to make *fewer* mistakes in the future! Venturing out from your comfort zone is one way to practice new judgments and make new mistakes. That's how you learn; it's that straightforward.

"If you use the same recipe, you get the same results."

—*Gerald Weinberg (b. 1933–2018)*

---

* Takeaway	"Good judgment comes from experience; experience comes from bad judgment."
	—*Anonymous*

* Take Action!	Write down two times when you used bad judgment. For each one, write three actions you will do differently next time.

7-12. SET PERSONAL BOUNDARIES AND EXPECTATIONS

Set clear, unambiguous personal boundaries, or others will set them for you. Define to yourself how you want to be treated and where you will or will not cross a line. A simple example: you decide you don't like a nickname that somehow always gets bestowed upon you. Speak up by saying, "I prefer to be called . . ."

Define for yourself your expectations for your relationships with friends, in your marriage, at work, or with anyone; otherwise others will define them for you. It takes time and experience with relationships to understand whether your expectations are being met. For example, an important quality in a friendship is others' willingness and ability to give honest, direct answers if you ask for advice. You probably don't want to hear what they think you want to hear.

* Takeaway	Define your boundaries and expectations for yourself and your life.
* Take Action!	Write down two times when you allowed someone to step over your personal boundaries. (If you don't have any personal boundaries now, create some first!) Then write three things you will do the next time it happens that will lead to a desirable outcome for you.

7-13. DIGNITY, HONOR, AND RESPECT

These three words are not very common these days. Treat yourself and others with dignity, honor, and respect, and for the most part, others will treat you the same way, especially if you set clear boundaries and expectations for how you want to be treated. The opposite is also true: if you treat yourself poorly, others will treat you the same way.

Do you have call-waiting on your phone? Unless you tell someone ahead of time that you're expecting a call, don't interrupt one call to take another. Do you have a mobile phone? Don't interrupt a conversation to take a call or respond to a text message. That's treating the person you're currently talking to without dignity, honor, or respect.

| * Takeaway | Treat yourself and others with dignity, honor, and respect, and most others will treat you the same way. |
| * Take Action! | Write down two times you allowed people to treat you without dignity, honor, or respect. Write three ways you will respond positively the next time similar situations arise. |

7-14. IMPOSSIBLE VS. POSSIBLE VS. HARD

As Andrew J. Galambos defined it, the term "impossible" means something that violates a law of nature. If something is possible, it might still be hard to achieve—or what's necessary to achieve it might not be known yet. Airplane flight was *possible* a thousand, a million, or a billion years ago, but it was only in 1903 that the Wright brothers presented the world with the knowledge needed to fly in a heavier-than-air machine.

| * Takeaway | There is a big difference between what is impossible and what might be hard to accomplish. |
| * Take Action! | Write two goals that you currently think are impossible for you to attain. Do they *really* violate any laws of nature? (Probably not.) Write what is *hard* about the goals and the first steps you will take toward achieving those goals. |

7-15. WOULD YOU GUARANTEE YOUR WORK?

Would you guarantee your work to your customer or employer? Maybe, maybe not, but internalizing a "satisfaction guaranteed" attitude creates a mind-set for superior work and self-responsibility. You will probably make mistakes, but if you guarantee your work, your customer or employer won't pay for them. Instead, *you* will pay for them. But you will also learn in the process what went wrong and what you can do better next time.

Consider return policies at retail stores that specify you can return certain products within a certain date. But what happens behind the scenes? The retail store returns the product to the manufacturer, who absorbs the loss. If that happens too often, the manufacturer may cancel production or the store may cease to carry the product.

There is also a cost to you for this "free" service. The retail store pays staff to manage the return process. That cost is built into the store's pricing.
Ponder this:

"Why is there time to do things over and not time to do them once right?"

—*Anonymous*

* Takeaway   Guaranteeing your work sets a high standard of quality and responsibility to strive for.

7-16. YET THERE ARE NO GUARANTEES IN LIFE

The horse and buggy preceded the car. Did we need laws then to guarantee the horse-and-buggy driver's income as cars emerged? Some jobs and products become obsolete as society and technology evolve. There is no guarantee that the career you choose will not become obsolete, so look ahead and prepare for change.
As mentioned earlier:

"The only constant in nature is change."

—*Heraclitus (ca. 535–475 BCE), ancient Greek philosopher*

"When you're finished changing, you're finished."

—*Benjamin Franklin (1706–1890)*

And on a humorous note:

"Men marry women with the hope they will never change. Women marry men with the hope they will change. Invariably they are both disappointed."

—*Albert Einstein (1879–1955)*

* Takeaway   Embrace change or be left behind; there are no guarantees in life.

* Take Action!   Write two ways you currently avoid change, and
                      why. Determine if the "why" is from fear or if you
                      really don't want to change!

7-17. IGNORANCE AND AWARENESS

One sign of adulthood is the ability to live with ambiguity. Kids learn from
various media that problems are resolved in a half hour or an hour. Life's
more ambiguous and complicated than that!

Table 7.1 shows how ignorance and awareness relate to ambiguity and
adulthood. First, here is how the Oxford English Dictionary defines the terms:

Ignorance   Lack of knowledge or information
Awareness   Knowledge or perception of a situation or fact

Table 7.1. Combining Ignorance and Awareness

	Unaware	Aware
Ignorant	Danger!!!	Welcome to adulthood (ambiguity)
Knowledgeable	You're better off than you think!	Can be satisfying, can be dangerous ☺

One of the (many?) reasons people often say they would never want to
relive their teen years is "I knew nothing then!" Sigh. Unaware *and* ignorant!
(There's a well-known bumper sticker: "Hire a teenager while they still know
everything.")

Sidebar: How ignorant were you three years ago compared with today?
So how much more knowledgeable do you think you'll be three years from
now? How will that happen? Answer for yourself what you specifically did
to acquire that new knowledge, including what didn't work. In other words,
review under what circumstances you practiced good and bad judgment.

* Takeaway   Being an adult means embracing ambiguity.
* Take Action!   Identify a situation you have now in which the am-
                      biguity is gnawing at you. Determine why you are
                      uncomfortable with the ambiguity and write three

steps you can take to accept or resolve the ambiguity. For example, are you now in a personal or business relationship with unclear boundaries? Write three ways to make the boundaries clear.

7-18. COMMON WORDS AND PHRASES TO RECONSIDER

Some common expressions can have a significant impact on your psyche without your awareness. Here are a few and what you can do about them.

"Woulda-Coulda-Shoulda" vs. "Next Time"

Saying "I should have" or its two partners (woulda, coulda) puts the focus on the unchangeable past. Instead, when you realize you made a mistake, say "Next time." This changes the focus to what you are capable of doing next time when faced with a similar situation. That's called "learning from experience" or "developing good judgment."

"I Have to" vs. "I Choose To"

You don't *have to* do anything. *Everything* you do is by choice. Stop saying "I have to" and start saying "I choose to." This teaches your brain to judge and to set priorities. One sobering thought, though:

"For every path you choose, there is another you must abandon, usually forever."

—Joan Vinge (b. 1948)

Accept Compliments Graciously

When someone compliments you, simply say thank you. Minimizing a compliment with comments like "Oh, it's nothing, really" or "This old dress?" insults the person giving the compliment—you're saying that person has poor judgment—and reduces yourself in your own eyes. (From www.waitley.com.) And just don't use the word "just"! It's a minimizer: "I've climbed *just* five Fourteeners." That's five more than the vast majority of people! Instead: "I've climbed *five* Fourteeners!"

"Are You Sure?"

Here's a related item. Say you're going to a movie with a friend and she of-fers to buy your ticket. A common response is, "Are you sure?" What you're actually doing is minimizing her offer and casting doubts on her judgment. If you want her to buy the ticket, accept graciously with a thank you. If you don't, decline graciously.

Don't "Try"—Just *Do*!

"Try" is a cop-out word. If you say, "I will try to study more," you are giving yourself an out. If you say, "I will study two hours a day," you are using com-mitment language and are more likely to succeed. Take a moment and say out loud the above two quoted sentences, emphasizing the word "will." You will feel positive emotions.

"Do or do not. There is no try."

—Yoda (b. A long time ago in a galaxy far, far away)

"Good" and "Bad"

"Good" and "bad" are the most subjective, judgmental words in the English language! They are loaded with individuals' personal perceptions and judg-ments. Clearly, what's good and bad for you might be completely different or even the opposite for someone else. So avoid using them whenever possible. For example, instead of, "That sounds like a good technique for writing," you can say, "That technique leads to clearer communication."

For a quirky example, what does "bad weather" mean? During Colorado winters, it sometimes does get cold, and it sometimes does snow. Is that "bad weather"? It's *weather*, period! You are perfectly capable of deciding what good and bad weather is! To many Coloradans (and a lot of tourists), snow is the ultimate blessing: skiing and snowboarding!

Pride

Consider these two questions:

Do you take pride in your local sports team?

Do you take pride in your personal accomplishments?

Do you see the difference between the origin of the pride in these two questions? For the former, you've probably done nothing to contribute to the team's wins. (Losses, of course, are their fault, right? Aren't the idioms "We won" but "They lost"?).

So is pride relevant? In the latter question, your efforts contributed to the accomplishments (if not, there's nothing to take pride in).

* Takeaway   Stay away from expressions that drag you down.

7-19. THE BEN FRANKLIN DECISION TOOL

When faced with several choices, consider this decision-making tool attributed to Benjamin Franklin. Create three columns on a blank sheet of paper or a computer:

1. The ideas or choices you are considering
2. Their pros—the reasons to select that choice
3. Their cons—the reasons to reject that choice

Dumping the ideas, the pros, and the cons from the brain and having all of them in full view gives you mental and emotional room to evaluate the options more clearly and reduces the anxiety of the unknown. Table 7.2 shows an example of this tool.

Table 7.2.   Example of the Ben Franklin Decision-Making Tools

	Evaluating Possible Jobs	
Job Search	Pros	Cons
Company 1	Great work; salary OK	Long commute
Company 2	Short commute; great people	Work is OK; low salary
Company 3	High salary	Lousy work
Company 4	High salary	No advancement

You can take this a step further, as shown in table 7.3, and assign weights to different criteria. A clear solution usually floats to the top. (Often, people go with their hearts anyway!)

Table 7.3. Example of the Ben Franklin Decision-Making Tools: Evaluating Possible Jobs with Weights Assigned

Job Search	Pros	Weight	Cons	Weight
Company 1	Great work;	5	Long	3
	salary OK	4	commute	
Company 2	Short commute;	3	Work is OK;	3
	great people	5	low salary	5
Company 3	High salary	4	Lousy work	1
Company 4	High salary	4	No advancement	1

The key is that you are not juggling emotion-laden thoughts in your mind that crowd out the ability to think clearly.

"Believe in yourself; everyone close to you already does."

—*Anonymous*

---

* Takeaway   The Ben Franklin decision tool helps compare contrasting choices.

* Take Action!   Do a "Ben Franklin" for a situation involving several choices that you have now. For example, are you considering graduate school, a job, or both at the same time? What are the pros and cons?

7-20. COMMON MISTAKES IN PERSONAL IMPROVEMENT

This is another topic for an entire book! But here are some common ones:

1. Not *choosing* how you feel but reacting to previous emotional scripts.
2. Reacting on impulse rather than responding thoughtfully to an unpleasant situation.
3. Using self-talk to reinforce unproductive behavior rather than to raise self-esteem.
4. Not setting clear, specific goals.
5. Dwelling on the past when making mistakes by choosing phrases like "I woulda-coulda-shoulda" instead of "Next time."
6. Feeling "I *have* to" instead of "I *choose* to."

TAKEAWAY SUMMARY

7-1. "When you're finished changing, you're finished."

7-2. Practice "I like myself!" at least five times a day. Out loud and with *feeling*!

7-3. Learn what your Emotional Intelligence is.

7-4. Use only positive, constructive self-talk.

7-5. You *can* grow your intelligence with a growth mind-set.

7-6. Work on weaknesses one at a time, converting them to strengths.

7-7. Set clear, specific goals with deadlines.

7-8. You *can* learn to respond positively to negative stressful situations.

7-9. Use the well-established system described in Mr. Allen's book.

7-10. Use a daily to-do list.

7-11. Good judgment comes from experience, which comes from bad judgment.

7-12. Define your boundaries and expectations for yourself and your life.

7-13. Treat yourself and others with dignity, honor, and respect, and most others will treat you the same way.

7-14. There is a big difference between what is impossible and what might be hard to accomplish.

7-15. Guaranteeing your work sets a high standard of quality and responsibility to strive for.

7-16. Embrace change or be left behind; there are no guarantees in life.

7-17. Being an adult means embracing ambiguity.

7-18. Stay away from expressions that drag you down.

7-19 The Ben Franklin decision tool helps compare contrasting choices.

8

Time Management

"The most productive day of the workweek is Tuesday."

—Source: *https://www.buzzfeednews.com/article/jessicamisener*

The main ideas to consider in managing time well are how to do the following:

- Be a hero and save people time.
- Be at least 10 percent more productive than your fellow coworkers.
- Balance urgency and importance.
- Seek balance in life.
- Learn your most productive times of the day.
- Respect your own time.
- Stay away from the domino effect of time wasters.
- Learn time management skills.
- Avoid common mistakes in time management.

8-1. BE A HERO: SAVE PEOPLE TIME!

If you're self-employed or work for a company, if you create a product or sell a service, or if you have people close to you, you'll be a hero if you save people time. Think of how often you've heard someone say, "I need more time in the day!"

Time is the *only* unrecoverable resource. Broken vases can be repaired or replaced; a lost day cannot. Keep this in mind, and you will focus on using time well, both for yourself and for those you interact with. This indirectly teaches you other positive habits:

1. Writing clearly, succinctly, and precisely so people quickly understand your intent.
2. Showing up early or on time for appointments.
3. Taking the time to do things once correctly, rather than doing them over and over.
4. Learning from others how they save time for themselves and others.

There's a saying in the computer programming world, "Weeks of programming can save you hours of planning." ☺

"Time is the coin of your life. It is the only coin you have, and only you can determine how it will be spent. Be careful lest you let other people spend it for you."

—Carl Sandburg (1878–1967)

"You may delay, but time will not."

—Benjamin Franklin (1706–1790)

---

* Takeaway   Be a hero and save people time.
* Take Action!   Think of one way you spent time recently with nothing to show for it. Write three things you can do next time instead of wasting the time.

8-2. HOW TO EASILY BE 10 PERCENT MORE PRODUCTIVE THAN YOUR COWORKERS

Be immediately 10 percent more productive than your coworkers by simply bringing your own meal and working through lunch! This gives you one more hour of productive time than your coworkers. You're transforming an eight-hour-plus-one-hour-for-lunch workday into a nine-hour workday. Without additional knowledge or skills, you become more than 10 percent more productive thanks to that extra hour. Your coworkers may comment on your antisocial behavior, so this approach might not work if having lunch with coworkers is important to you. (Also be sure to check that the practice of working through lunch is legal in your state. Seriously.)

| * Takeaway | Work through lunch and save socializing for after work. |

8-3. URGENCY AND IMPORTANCE

Table 8.1 shows a simple tool to help your mind blend urgent and important matters.

Table 8.1. Deciding Urgency vs. Importance

Urgency vs. Importance	Not Important	Important
Not Urgent	Do you really have to do it?	Source of progress
Urgent	Why not delay or skip it?	Deal with it now!

When deciding whether to do something, determine its urgency and importance accordingly. Separating paper clips by color can usually wait. If you get a work assignment that is, in your assessment, urgent but not important, discuss it with your boss or coworkers to determine whether or when the work should be done.

"Never confuse motion with action."

—*Benjamin Franklin (1706–1790)*

| * Takeaway | Ensure importance is a factor in decision making, not just urgency. |

8-4. BALANCE IN LIFE

As noted in the previous section, there will always be pressing important and urgent matters. Health aside, most things in life can usually wait, and the world will not come to an end if you delay some tasks. Facing a pressing deadline? Renegotiate with the people involved. Can't pay a bill that's due? Renegotiate with the people or company involved. Missed attaining a goal you had set? Welcome to the human race. Reexamine the "goals of the goal" (why did you set the goal?) to determine whether it was realistic or even desirable. If yes, set a new target date. If not, examine why you didn't attain the goal; maybe you didn't want it after all, so create new ones.

Balance in life is highly personal, so this is all we'll cover on the subject. There are terabytes of information to explore. See www.nightingale.com and look at the "Categories" tab for material.

* Takeaway   To maintain balance, find activities (including doing nothing) that soothe your mind.

8-5. WHAT ARE YOUR PRODUCTIVE TIMES OF DAY?

Determine what times of day you are most and least productive and adjust your work and play schedules accordingly.

* Takeaway   Guard your productive times of the day from misuse by you or others!

8-6. RESPECT YOUR OWN TIME

Respect your own time and learn to say no! When you keep your goals in mind, it's a lot easier to say no to people, including yourself, who may be tempting you with a misuse of your time. Are your goals more important than a distraction from them?

* Takeaway   If you respect your and others' time, most others will respect yours.

8-7. TIME *IS* MONEY!

How do you "find the time" to go after your goals? How about spending less time with your mobile phone or video games? Figure 8.1 has a spreadsheet that shows that time is, indeed, money. The cells in column B, rows 8–13, are assumed time in minutes you can save if you use (that is, play with) your phone less. The cells in columns E, F, and G show annual time savings in minutes, hours, and days, respectively. Column H shows how that time represents money by placing a value of $10 an hour (cell F3) on the time. Column I has the amount of money saved over forty years, while column J shows that same amount invested at a monthly compounded rate of 5 percent for forty years.

For example, with these numbers, saving thirty minutes a day (whether by reduced mobile-phone usage or any other way) can yield $228,903.02.

A	B	C	D	E	F	G	H	I	J
1	Time Is Money - How much is your time worth?								
2									
3	30	days/month		$10.00	per hour			40	years of compounding
4								5.0%	Interest rate (annual)
5	Daily	Weekly	Monthly	ANNUAL SAVINGS			Annual		Annual Value
6	Minutes	Minutes	Minutes				Dollar	Over	Compounded
7	Saved	Saved	Saved	Minutes	Hours	Days	Value	40 Years	Monthly @ 5%
8	5	35	150	1,800	30	1 1/4	$300	$12,000	$38,150.50
9	10	70	300	3,600	60	2 1/2	$600	$24,000	$76,301.01
10	15	105	450	5,400	90	3 3/4	$900	$36,000	$114,451.51
11	20	140	600	7,200	120	5	$1,200	$48,000	$152,602.02
12	25	175	750	9,000	150	6 1/4	$1,500	$60,000	$190,752.52
13	30	210	900	10,800	180	7 1/2	$1,800	$72,000	$228,903.02

FIGURE 8.1. Demonstrate That Time Is Money

Table 8.2 shows the yield of saving thirty minutes a day for two hourly rates and three interest rates.

Table 8.2. Sample Yields of Money Saved over Forty Years

Hourly Rate	Interest	Yield	Difference
$10.00	5%	$228,903.02	—
	8%	$523,651.17	$294,748.15
	10%	$948,611.94	$424,960.77
$20.00	5%	$457,806.05	—
	8%	$1,047,302.35	$589,496.30
	10%	$1,897,223.87	$849,921.52

Compare the lines with $10 an hour and interest rates of 8 percent and 10 percent. The 2 percent difference in the rate over forty years yields an additional $424,960.77, almost half a million dollars! That's the power of compound interest. (See idea 10-8 for more discussion of compound interest.) Does this affect your view on your use of time? If you *do* save the time shown here, will you use it in a beneficial way? If not, you haven't saved a second.

    * Takeaway   Keep your mobile phone on silent and check it only a few times a day. Very few situations are so urgent that they need immediate attention.

* Take Action!   Decide now to find thirty minutes a day by reduc-
                           ing wasted time. Start by using (playing with) your
                           mobile phone less.

8-8. TIME-SAVING FILING TIP

Whether with paper or on a computer, don't use a category or folder named
"Miscellaneous" or you'll find everything ends up there. Take the initial time
to prepare filing categories that are relevant to your situation.

8-9. DUMP, DELAY, DO, OR DELEGATE

One legacy of the Apollo space program and Apollo 11's landing on the moon
is advances in project management. One Apollo project manager developed
the "Dump, Delay, Do, or Delegate" approach to handling tasks on a project:

Dump	Don't do the task! It might be unnecessary or no longer relevant.
Delay	Do the task later.
Do	Do the task now and complete it.
Delegate	Delegate the task to someone else. Younger siblings are convenient. ☺

8-10. COMMON MISTAKES IN TIME MANAGEMENT

Often, people are:

1. Not using prioritized daily to-do lists.
2. Treating urgency and importance at the same level when deciding what
   to do next.
3. Wasting the productive times of day.
4. Overemphasizing work or play.
5. Squandering time through unnecessary activities.

TAKEAWAY SUMMARY

8-1. Be a hero and save people time.
8-2. Work through lunch and save socializing for after work.
8-3. Ensure importance is a factor in decision making, not just urgency.

8-4. To maintain balance, find activities (including doing nothing) that soothe your mind.

8-5. Guard your productive times of the day from misuse by you or others!

8-6. If you respect your and others' time, most others will respect yours.

8-7. Keep your mobile phone on silent and check it only a few times a day. Very few situations are so urgent that they need immediate attention.

9

A View of Corporate America

"Few of us can stand prosperity. Another man's, I mean."

—*Mark Twain (1835–1910)*

The main ideas to consider while discussing Corporate America are how to do the following:

- Define what Corporate America is.
- Understand the basics of Corporate America by examining a company.
- Prevent yourself from getting ripped off.
- Know the concepts of risk and reward.
- Grasp "fair compensation."
- Recognize the meaning of "greed" and "free."
- Learn how profit is used.
- Avoid common misconceptions about Corporate America.

9-1. THE MAIN REASON FOR THIS CHAPTER

The main reason for this chapter, which explains some of the workings of Corporate America, is to apply idea 3-2, "Don't Categorize People," to companies. As with people, there are "good" companies and "bad" companies, but neither defines the majority of companies.

9-2. WHAT IS "CORPORATE AMERICA"?

As of this writing (December 2019), roughly 129 million people are employed by the private sector. (See the Bureau of Labor Statistics data at http://data.bls .gov/timeseries/CES0500000001.)

Of that number, tens of millions work for Corporate America, so it helps to understand what Corporate America is and how it works. Here is a simple definition: the collection of large profit-seeking companies in the private sector in America. "Large" is left to your imagination. These companies have several common characteristics. They

1. are in business to supply products and services;
2. employ thousands to millions of people;
3. use several layers of management;
4. have offices located in many cities (and in many cases, countries);
5. seek to make a profit; and
6. exhibit a corporate culture that is usually known to the public.

9-3. PERCEPTIONS OF CORPORATE AMERICA

Corporate America is typically portrayed by the media as headed by ruthless, heartless swindlers who are out to rip everyone off and screw the world. Yes, there are people like that (including in the media!), but they are a small minority. Think of the companies that supply the products and services you buy and use every day, such as food and clothing. Are they really in business *just* to rip you off? Unlikely. If you think so, what can you do? In this great land of choice, America, you can always take your business elsewhere.

Google "top companies to work for in the U.S." (or in the area where you live) to view a list of companies that people enjoy working for. Some you may not have even heard of.

Sidebar: It is ironically amusing that movies from Hollywood studios often portray Corporate America in a negative light while ignoring the fact that Hollywood is part of Corporate America. Think of the "Hollywood lifestyle" and the amounts of money associated with it.

Small businesses are not part of Corporate America by definition, but how are they perceived? Are small-business owners that you encounter every day generally pleasant or nasty? Do they seem glad to be where they are, or are they shooting daggers at you with their eyes while thinking about how to rip you off? And what can you do if you don't like the product or service of a small business? In this great land of choice, America, you can always take your business elsewhere.

According to the Small Business Administration's 2018 report, there are 30.2 million small businesses in America comprising 99.9% of all American businesses, but we won't explore small business further in this chapter. (For the full report, see https://www.sba.gov/sites/default/files/advocacy/2018 -Small-Business-Profiles-US.pdf.)

* Takeaway	Corporate America includes "good" companies, "bad" companies, and everything in between.
* Take Action!	Find three companies near where you live that are rated desirable to work for.

9-4. A LOOK AT ONE COMPANY IN CORPORATE AMERICA

This section examines a well-known company. You decide if they are ripping you and the public off.

What do you think of a company that every second earns $594.20 in sales, with a profit of $169.94? Yes, every *second*. Its profits in the second calendar quarter of 2019 (April 1–June 30) were $1.3361 billion. Revenue for this quarter was $4.6718 billion. Here's what $4.6718 billion in one quarter looks like as a number: $4,671,800,000. That is a large number! So is $51,338,461.54, which is the revenue *per day* for the quarter.

Figure 9.1 shows these quarterly results broken down to sales and profits per day, hour, minute, and second.

A	B	C	D	E	F	G
1		2019, 2nd Quarter	For unit figures, divide the column to its left by:			
2	Dates:	Apr 1, 2019	91	24	60	60
3	(91 Days)	Jun 30, 2019	Per Day	Per Hour	Per Minute	Per Second
4	Sales	$4,671,800,000.00	$51,338,461.54	$2,139,102.56	$35,651.71	$594.20
5	Profit	$1,336,100,000.00	$14,682,417.58	$611,767.40	$10,196.12	$169.94

FIGURE 9.1. Second-Quarter 2019 Corporate Earnings for a Mystery Corporation

That's right! The company sold its products at a rate of $594.20 *per second* and earned a net profit of $169.94 *per second*. The net-profit percentage is profit divided by sales multiplied by 100, or $(169.94 \div 594.20) \times 100 = 28.60$

percent net profit during that quarter. Stated another way, every dollar in sales yielded 28.60 cents in profit. Not bad!

Are you surprised to learn the company is Starbucks? Is Starbucks ripping you off? Read the next section and decide for yourself.

Data source: https://investor.starbucks.com/press-releases/financial -releases/press-release-details/2019/Starbucks-Reports-Q3-Fiscal-2019 -Results/.

* Takeaway	Companies grow by reinvesting their profits. (Well, that's not *really* in this section, but that's a major use for profits.)
* Take Action!	Search the web for the quarterly or annual profits of companies you know. How many of these companies have losses? Why do you think that is?

9-5. DOES CORPORATE AMERICA RIP YOU OFF?

First of all, what is meant by the term "to rip off"? Here are a few definitions:

1. Merriam-Webster: "to cheat, defraud."
2. TheFreeDictionary.com: "(a) to steal from; (b) to exploit, swindle, cheat or defraud."
3. Dictionary.Reference.com: "(a) to steal or pilfer; (b) to rob or steal from; (c) to swindle, cheat, or exploit; take advantage of."

So is Starbucks ripping you off? Absolutely not! You *always* have a choice to buy at Starbucks or not to buy at Starbucks. (You don't *need* Starbucks to survive.) That is true of the vast majority of the purchases you make. You can also choose not to buy at all (see "Wants vs. Needs" in idea 10-2). Put another way, if you feel you're about to get ripped off, simply don't buy the product or service (or sign an agreement). Instead, contact the company and express your opinion of its prices.

So how often does Corporate America truly rip you off? Are corporations really ripping you off, or are you in a situation in which you buy when you think you really shouldn't because the product or service is inferior? Then simply don't buy. You can also take this one step further: If you think you can do something better than another person or company, start a company and compete!

You always have a choice when dealing with a company. This translates to: You vote every day with your wallet. You can also vote with your pen, keyboard, or mobile phone. Unhappy with a company's product or service? Write or call and let them know! By the way, you can also write or call a company to let them know you're pleased with their products or services. Goodwill goes a long way in both directions.

* Takeaway	You can avoid getting ripped off by making different choices.
* Take Action!	If you think a company is ripping you off, look elsewhere for a similar product or service. Let the company know why you are looking elsewhere.

9-6. RISK AND REWARD

What does it take to generate a profit? It takes knowledge of the business, the marketplace, and the company's operations. And, of course, it takes risks. "Take a risk, earn a reward." Profit is a reward for taking a risk. The greatest critics of companies are typically people who have never run one. It takes a lot of sustained hard work by many people to produce a profit honestly, *especially* when customers always have the choice to go elsewhere.

If, by your own determination (and not what others tell you), you don't like what a company does for a living, don't buy their products or services. One way to get companies to change direction is to let them know why you're not buying their products or services.

* Takeaway	Profit is the reward for taking healthy risks. Loss is an outcome that is a learning experience.

9-7. WHAT IS FAIR COMPENSATION?

Just what *is* "fair compensation"? Plain and simple, compensation is fair if you choose to agree to a compensation offer. If you don't like something about a contract—that is, you think it's not fair—either attempt to renegotiate the terms or don't enter into it. Plain and simple.

What is your concept of fair compensation? Why? *Who* decides what is fair? For that matter, what does "fair" mean? Are sports salaries fair? Why or why not? In 2019, Los Angeles Dodger pitcher Clayton Kershaw earned $31,000,000 for the 162-game season. Table 9.1 shows what that $31,000,000 looks like if we break it down using Mr. Kershaw's statistics for the 2019 season.

Table 9.1.   Clayton Kershaw Compensation 2019

Los Angeles Dodger's Clayton Kershaw 2019 Annual Compensation			$31,000,000.00
Line	Statistical Category	Number	Salary per Number
1	Starts	28	$1,107,142.86
2	Pitches	2,672	$11,601.80
3	Wins	16	$1,937,500.00
4	Batters Faced	706	$43,909.35

Line 4 in Table 9.1 is nothing short of astounding. Mr. Kershaw earned $43,909.35 every time he faced a batter. Is that fair to Mr. Kershaw? To the Dodgers? Yes, it is, because they both agreed to it. Is that fair to anyone else? It's no one else's business, so it doesn't matter if anyone else thinks it's fair. By the way, this is not intended to praise, critique, or condemn Mr. Kershaw's salary; this is merely what you see when you look at his compensation from a different perspective.

* Takeaway	"Fair compensation" is highly subjective. Each person must make an individual choice.
* Take Action!	Find out typical salaries for work or careers you're considering. Do they seem fair to you? Why or why not? One resource for determining salaries is http://www.roberthalf.com/salary-guides. (Part of Robert Half International's excellent reputation comes from its compilation of salary surveys.)

9-8. "YOUR FAIR SHARE"

Now be prepared for several rhetorical questions.

What does "your fair share" mean? What is your "fair share" of what someone else has worked for and earned? On what basis do you know? How do you calculate it? Who decides what's fair? How? Why?

Regarding income taxes, do you maximize your tax deductions to minimize your income tax payments? Or do you pay "your fair share" and maximize your income tax payments? Whichever you do, why do you do it? Are you being fair to the U.S. government?

In the 1960s, the writers at *Mad* magazine developed a marvelous solution to government taxing and spending: when you mail in your income tax payment, you specify how you want the money to be spent, much as people decide how to allocate their household budget. For some reason, the idea was never adopted.

    * Takeaway   "Your fair share" is what you earn.

9-9. GREED AND "FREE"

This quote summarizes what many people think about personal and corporate greed:

"Why is it greedy to hold on to what you earned, but not greedy to want what someone else has earned?"

—Thomas Sowell (b. 1930)

It's noteworthy that stories of corporate greed make the news occasionally, as do stories of airplane crashes. Both happen, but not as often as the media lead us to believe. Most companies are out there to make a reasonable profit providing a useful product or service.

If greed is a factor, it often rules both sides of a transaction: one person offering a deal seemingly too good to be true finds another person who wants something too good to be true.

Related to this is the concept of "free." Nothing is free; *everything* has a cost. Toll-free numbers are not free. Free samples are not free. Companies or individuals offering toll-free numbers and "free" samples build the costs of their "freebies" into their products or services, so we all pay for them indirectly.

Robert A. Heinlein (1907–1988), author of *Stranger in a Strange Land* and other science fiction classics, created the acronym TANSTAAFL: "There ain't no such thing as a free lunch." There's *always* a cost. The crucial questions are always who pays, how much, why, when, and for how long.

"Free" really means "at no direct cost to you now, but at some cost to you or other people now or later."

| * Takeaway | TANSTAAFL: There ain't no such thing as a free lunch. |

9-10. WHAT SHOULD COMPANIES DO WITH THEIR PROFITS?

British comedian Russell Brand said in a 2013 interview with the BBC: "Where there's profit, there's deficit. Profit is a filthy word." By the way, he was worth $15 million at the time and has yet to distribute fair shares of it.

The Oxford English Dictionary defines profit as "a financial gain, esp. the difference between the amount earned and the amount spent in buying, operating, or producing something." So profit can mean a deficit if the company loses money. But what is filthy about this definition?

Minute One of Day One of Business 101 talks of the *necessity* of profit for businesses to survive and, yes, flourish.

So what should companies do with their profits? Answer: whatever they want. Most companies earn them honestly and use them to expand the products and services they offer, leading to more choices for you.

| * Takeaway | A company's profit is the company's to decide how to use. |
| * Take Action! | If you don't like how a company is using its profits, let them know. Challenge them to explain their reasons (though it really is none of your business). |

9-11. IF YOU HAVE A COMPLAINT WITH A COMPANY

If you have a complaint with a company, take it straight to the highest-ranking person who has the authority to deal with the problem. This will save you the time of dealing with layers of management and having to repeat your story eighteen times. Most websites have a "Contact Us" link, so find the company's phone number, call (don't waste time with e-mail), and ask to speak immediately to someone at a management level. You might be asked to explain the problem first, but you usually don't have to if you're adamant.

> * Takeaway   Take complaints about a company immediately to the highest-ranking manager you can find.

9-12. "LAST CHANCE TO SEND $1!"

There's a story about a guy who placed an ad in a newspaper. The ad merely said, "Last chance to send $1!" and listed a PO box address. He received more than $70,000! Did he rip those people off? No, because *all* respondents had a choice whether to respond. Read more about it at http://msgboard.snopes .com/cgi-bin/ultimatebb.cgi?ubb=get_topic;f=80;t=000568;p=1.

Apparently this type of ad was banned. But why pass a law? Why not let people learn from their mistakes if they want nothing for their $1?

While on the topic, watch out for advertisers who say, "Be one of the first one hundred callers!" and don't offer anything if you call!

> * Takeaway   Look carefully at offers, especially ones that appear too good to be true, because they usually are.

9-13. COMMON MISTAKES ABOUT CORPORATE AMERICA

Some common mistakes people make about Corporate America are:

1. Not understanding the role and importance of profit.
2. Assuming "free" means "at no cost."
3. Not understanding the complexities of how businesses operate efficiently and effectively.
4. Lumping good companies in with bad and annoying ones.

TAKEAWAY SUMMARY

9-2. Corporate America includes "good" companies, "bad" companies, and everything in between.

9-4. Companies grow by reinvesting their profits.

9-5. You can avoid getting ripped off by making different choices.

9-6. Profit is the reward for taking healthy risks. Loss is an outcome that is a learning experience.

9-7. "Fair compensation" is highly subjective. Each person must make an individual choice.

9-8. "Your fair share" is what you earn.

9-9. TANSTAAFL: There ain't no such thing as a free lunch.

9-10. A company's profit is the company's to decide how to use.

9-11. Take complaints about a company immediately to the highest-ranking manager you can find.

9-12. Look carefully at offers, especially ones that appear too good to be true, because they usually are.

10

Wealth and Finances

The main ideas to consider while learning about wealth, finances, and investing are how to do the following:

- Decide what wealth means to you.
- Separate wants vs. needs.
- Set a wealth bar for yourself.
- Get started building wealth.
- Speedily increase the amount in your savings account.
- Establish and keep a budget.
- Harness the power of compound interest.
- Manage cash and credit cards.
- Track your credit score.
- Avoid common mistakes about wealth and finances.

10-1. WHAT IS WEALTH?

What does wealth mean to you? As has been pointed out in many sections, if you don't decide for yourself on any matter, others will decide for you, and you'll live someone else's dream. Here are some concepts and definitions of wealth to help you hone your concept of it:

1. Merriam-Webster: "(a) a large amount of money and possessions; (b) the value of all the property, possessions, and money that someone or something has."

   Definition (a) uses "large," but (b) doesn't. So (b) can be used to measure positive *or* negative wealth and can include adjectives like "tiny," "small," "medium," "large," or "humongous" (or any other adjective you want to use).

2. Wikipedia: "The abundance of valuable resources or material possessions."

3. Investopedia.com: "A measure of the value of all of the assets of worth owned by a person, community, company, or country. Wealth is determined by adding up the total market value of all the physical and intangible assets of the entity and subtracting all debts."

   Investopedia's definition of wealth is similar to net worth and, like the Merriam-Webster definition, allows for wealth of all sizes, positive or negative.

4. R. Buckminster Fuller (1895–1983), a futurist, inventor, and architect who created the geodesic dome and popularized the term "Spaceship Earth," had this concept of wealth: the measure of the ability to control your future.

   By Fuller's definition, a person who has a net worth of $1 billion and stage 4 terminal cancer is not wealthy. A person with a net worth of $1,000 who can choose how to spend his or her day is wealthier. Note how time plays such a vital role in this concept.

If any of these definitions is useful to you, great. If not, create your own. Will you decide for yourself what wealth means to you, or will you let someone else (or society) define it for you?

"Wealth is not his that has it, but his that enjoys it."

—*Benjamin Franklin (1706–1790)*

"Who is rich? One who is happy with his lot."

—*Shimon ben Zoma (ca. second century CE), Pirkei Avot 4:1*

| * Takeaway | You get to decide what wealth means to you. |
| * Take Action! | Decide what wealth means to you, whether in words, dollars, possessions, balance of life, use of time, or some combination of these. |

10-2. WANTS VS. NEEDS

Question: What do you truly *need* to survive? Answer: food, water, clothing, and, in nontropical climates, shelter. Anything else is a *want*. It's a simple distinction. Recall the discussion of gratitude in idea 3-4. A helpful way to set your attitude every morning is to be aware and grateful that you have met your needs. Everything else is gravy.

Now tie this concept to Fuller's concept of wealth. How much do you truly need to be happy? How much is enough? And how do your needs and wants tie into your personal definition of success? These are powerful questions; take the time to answer them.

Sidebar: As comedian Steven Wright (b. 1955) once noted in his usual deadpan manner, "You can't have everything. Where would you put it?"

| * Takeaway | There are very few "needs"; most things are "wants," which are choices. |
| * Take Action! | Make an honest list of your needs and wants. How do they dovetail with the concept of wealth you developed with idea 10-1? List your "wants" in order of most to least wanted. What will you do (or pass up) to acquire your "wants" and increase your wealth? |

10-3. SETTING YOUR WEALTH BAR

Right out of college, would you be happy with a salary of $100,000 a year? Be honest, of course you would! How about $99,000 a year? Or $98,000? OK, how about $10,000 a year? Then your wealth bar is somewhere in between.

Your wealth bar is the starting salary you'd work for. Once a salary is set, it is difficult to get *major* increases, so decide carefully. You always have other options, such as looking for a job at a higher salary, pursuing promotions, or starting your own business.

* Takeaway	*You* decide (choose) your worth.
* Take Action!	Find out what you are worth in the marketplace before deciding what a fair compensation is.

10-4. HOW TO START SAVING MONEY

With all the fiscal responsibilities you have now, how can you start to build wealth? Simple. Andrew J. Galambos recommended George S. Clason's short book, titled *The Richest Man in Babylon*. First published in 1926 from a collection of pamphlets, it has simple, sound, and timeless principles for saving and investing money. Here are two of the book's key principles:

1. Pay yourself first into a savings account. Save 10 percent off the top of everything you earn. Yes, *everything*. If your salary is $500 a pay period, save $50; if it's $1,000 a pay period, save $100; if it's $2,718 a pay period, save $271.80. Putting this amount away is an easy way to start accumulating money. Another way of looking at this principle is that you live off 90 percent of your income. If you live off of 100 percent of your income, you will never get started accumulating wealth.
2. Get out of debt. Here's how:
    a. First, pay yourself 10 percent of your earnings and put it into savings (see above).
    b. Next, pay 20 percent of your earnings to your debtors. For credit card debt, set a goal to pay more than the minimum monthly payment. This will save you thousands of dollars of interest in the long run.
    c. Last, live off the remaining 70 percent of your income.

This approach ensures debt will be paid down. Debt doesn't just "go away." Once you are out of debt, you will be used to living on a smaller amount and can start saving much more than 10 percent of your income.

You can think of this savings account as your "Arkad account," after the character Arkad, the "richest man in Babylon" portrayed in *The Richest Man in Babylon*. This continuously reminds you of the main purpose of the account.

| * Takeaway | It's tough to start building wealth until you start saving money. |
| * Take Action! | Save at least 10 percent of everything you earn starting now. Pay down debt or it won't go away. |

10-5. HOW TO INCREASE YOUR SAVINGS ACCOUNT BALANCE QUICKLY

Growing your Arkad account is a state of mind, and you can make a game of it. Here are some ways to increase it faster:

1. Did you buy something on sale? Deposit the difference between the retail price and the sale price into your Arkad account. Otherwise, what have you really saved?
2. If you use store coupons, do the same thing: siphon off the difference between the retail prices and the discounted prices and put it into a cookie jar.
3. Dump loose change into the same cookie jar and deposit the contents into your Arkad account once a month.
4. Cheat! When it's time to calculate 10 percent of your income for savings, use 11 or 12 percent. Or round the number up to the nearest $10, $25, $50, or $100. Or both. You won't miss that little extra, and your Arkad account will grow faster.
5. While shopping, compare unit costs among products or different sizes of the same product. The largest box does not necessarily have the lowest unit price.
6. Save paper, money, and trash the next time you give a gift by not wrapping it. Think of how much wrapping paper is trashed, especially around birthdays and holidays.

| * Takeaway | Small savings here and there accumulate into large ones. |
| * Take Action! | Start saving *today* by using all or some of the tactics listed here and ones of your own. |

10-6. DEBT REDUCTION AND ELIMINATION

School loans? Credit card debt? Other debt? Dave Ramsey has ideas for you to stably get out of debt. Mr. Ramsey is a nationally syndicated radio talk show host, author, and financial guru. One of his businesses is Financial Peace University (FPU; www.daveramsey.com/FPU). And one of FPU's programs teaches how to budget, set up a beginner emergency fund, get out of debt, establish a full-fledged emergency fund, and invest for future wealth. FPU has many other classes geared to entrepreneurship, college-aged students, and general tips on getting out of debt. As of this writing, the price is $129.99 for a *family*, not an individual.

The website www.everydollar.com has a budgeting tool at no charge. Set up an initial budget in less than 15 minutes and get started in knowing where and how you spend your money.

* Takeaway	There are methodical ways to get out of debt.
* Take Action!	1. Visit www.daveramsey.com and www.daveramsey.com/FPU. Take action and enroll in the Financial Peace University's first course.
	2. Create a budget at www.everydollar.com. Stick to it!

10-7. ESTABLISHING CREDIT

Yes, it is difficult to establish credit with little income and a lot of debt. One way to establish credit is to obtain a secured credit card. With such a card, you pay into the card, and your credit limit is however much money you put into the account. If you pay off the balance monthly, you are on your way to establishing credit. The website www.creditkarma.com has no fees and has suggestions on getting secure credit cards. You can also get your FICO credit score at no charge.

* Takeaway	Establish credit with one or more secure credit cards.
* Take Action!	Visit www.creditkarma.com to start establishing credit.

10-8. THE POWER OF COMPOUND INTEREST

OK, so you started saving money. What are some options for growing that investment into much larger sums? Figure 10.1 shows three examples of the power of compound interest when investing $50, $100, and $150 a month for forty years. These three numbers are shown in parentheses, indicating negative amounts. (By commonly accepted accounting standards, negatives mean outgoing money.) The figure also shows how many $4 lattes a week or month one can forgo to accumulate such large sums of money. Forgoing three or four lattes a week frees up $50 a month to save and invest. See www.bankrate .com for a variety of financial-calculation tools.

	A	B	C	D	E	F	G	H	I	J	K	L
2			$12	Compounding periods a year				10	Increment of years			
3			$0	Initial deposit				1.5%	Increment of APR			
4												
5		#	Annual Percentage Rate									
6		Years	0%	1.5%	3.0%	4.5%	6.0%	7.5%	9.0%	10.5%	12.0%	
7			($50.00)	Monthly deposit amount								
8		10	$6,000	$6,469	$6,987	$7,559	$8,193	$8,896	$9,675	$10,540	$11,501	
9		20	$12,000	$13,984	$16,415	$19,406	$23,102	$27,686	$33,394	$40,525	$49,462	
10		30	$18,000	$22,714	$29,136	$37,969	$50,225	$67,372	$91,537	$125,820	$174,748	
11		40	$24,000	$32,857	$46,302	$67,057	$99,574	$151,191	$234,066	$368,452	$588,238	
12												
13			($100.00)	Monthly deposit amount								
14		10	$12,000	$12,938	$13,974	$15,119	$16,387	$17,793	$19,351	$21,081	$23,003	
15		20	$24,000	$27,968	$32,830	$38,812	$46,204	$55,373	$66,788	$81,050	$98,925	
16		30	$36,000	$45,429	$58,273	$75,938	$100,451	$134,744	$183,074	$251,640	$349,496	
17		40	$48,000	$65,714	$92,605	$134,115	$199,149	$302,382	$468,132	$736,904	$1,176,477	
18												
19			($150.00)	Monthly deposit amount								
20		10	$18,000	$19,407	$20,961	$22,679	$24,581	$26,689	$29,027	$31,622	$34,505	
21		20	$36,000	$41,952	$49,245	$58,218	$69,306	$83,059	$100,183	$121,575	$148,388	
22		30	$54,000	$68,144	$87,410	$113,907	$150,677	$202,116	$274,611	$377,460	$524,244	
23		40	$72,000	$98,572	$138,908	$201,172	$298,723	$453,573	$702,198	$1,105,356	$1,764,715	

FIGURE 10.1. Compound Interest Comparison Summary

For example, saving $50 a month for forty years at 5 percent annually, compounded monthly, yields $76,301. Make that $100 a month for forty years at 5 percent and the yield is $316,203, or a whopping 314 percent more! And $150 a month yields $1,550,802, or 1,932 percent more! Such is the power of compound interest. The same percentage increases apply to money invested at 10 percent and 15 percent. So merely by forgoing a few lattes a week, you can get started establishing and increasing savings.

Figure 10.2 shows some combinations of the same monthly amounts but with a range of years and interest rates.

Monthly	# Years	5.0%	10.0%	15.0%	Lattes/Month	Lattes/Week	Cost/Latte
($50)	40	$76,301	$152,602	$228,903	12.5	3.1	$4.00
($100)	40	$316,203	$632,407	$948,611	25.0	6.3	
($150)	40	$1,550,802	$3,101,605	$4,652,408	37.5	9.4	

FIGURE 10.2. Compound Interest Comparison Details

| * Takeaway | Time is on your side with the power of compound interest. |
| * Take Action! | Decide on a monthly amount to put aside starting *now*. |

10-9. "BUT LATER THE MONEY WON'T BE WORTH MUCH!"

A common first reaction when considering, say, that $100 a month can grow to hundreds of thousands of dollars over a few decades is, "But the money won't be worth much by then!" *But you'll have it!* If you don't save anything, you won't have it, plain and simple.

| * Takeaway | Growing money with compound interest means you have the money later, even if it's worth less. |

10-10. KEEP A BUDGET

Keep a budget to know your weekly, monthly, quarterly, and annual revenue and expenses. Monthly expenses have two broad categories: fixed and variable. Examples of fixed expenses are rent and bills for your cell phone (with no overage ☺) and internet connection. Variable expenses include gas and electric bills and gifts for special occasions, because they vary from month to month.

One key budgeting aspect often overlooked is preparing for recurring large expenses that occur only a few times a year, like car insurance and vacations. Let's take car insurance, which is often paid every six months. If that premium is, say, $720, put away in a savings account $720 ÷ 6 = $120 every month. When the bill is due, you'll have the money and won't have to scramble to pay it or lose your insurance. Keep a separate savings account—you may as well earn some interest—from the Arkad account, as the former will fluctuate, but the latter should just keep growing.

Once you've established a budget, here's how to limit your credit card use: on Sundays, withdraw the cash you project you'll use based on your budget for the coming week. Don't use credit cards, just cash. When you see cash leaving your wallet or purse, you feel as if you are spending money. That feeling is often lost when using credit cards, causing spending increases, so avoid using cards whenever possible.

There are hundreds of ways to do a budget, one of which is shown in the next section. The software product Quicken, by Intuit (www.intuit.com), has a powerful budgeting component and integrates well with expense tracking, check-register maintenance, credit card management, and online banking. (More in ideas 10-11 and 10-12.) Another excellent tool is the website www.mint.com, which runs in the Cloud and has no additional cost. Also check out the wide range of books by Suze Orman, one of which focuses on young adults: *The Money Book for the Young, Fabulous and Broke.*

* Takeaway	Keeping a budget helps increase savings and control expenses.
* Take Action!	Create a budget *today*!

10-11. BUDGETING TOOLS

You have many choices for budgeting tools, some of which are listed in this section. The first one is the one most recommended, as it includes budgeting that ties directly to your cash and credit card management, online reconciliation with your bank, investment management, and more.

1. The software package Quicken, by Intuit, discussed further in idea 10-14 on "Cash and Credit Card Management."
2. The Cloud service Mint (www.mint.com).
3. Any budgeting tool by Suze Orman, who also has several books on financial management and planning.

* Takeaway	Consider using a software product or app to manage your budget.
* Take action!	Start a budget *now*. See idea 10-11 for budgeting resources.

10-12. KEY IDEAS FOR A BUDGET

Figure 10.3 has a sample budget. Following the sample budget in figure 10.3 are interpretations and key ideas when using a budget. (All numbers are made up and are not meant to suggest that any income or expense dollar amount is an actual amount.) The most complicated math you'll need is the ability to calculate percentages.

	A	B	C	D	E	F	G	H	I	J	K	L	M	N	O
1			Total	Apr	May	Jun	Jul	Aug	Sep	Oct	Nov	Dec	Jan	Feb	Mar
2		Gross Income													
3		Primary Job	10,000	800	800	800	800	800	800	800	800	900	900	900	900
4		Supplemental 1	2,600	300	300	200	300	300	300	300				300	300
5		Total Gross	12,600	1,100	1,100	1,000	1,100	1,100	1,100	1,100	800	900	900	1,200	1,200
6															
7		Net Income													
8	80%	Primary Job	8,000	640	640	640	640	640	640	640	640	720	720	720	720
9	84%	Supplemental 1	2,184	252	252	168	252	252	252	252				252	252
10		Total Net	10,184	892	892	808	892	892	892	892	640	720	720	972	972
11															
12		Expenses													
13		Fixed													
14	10%	Savings	1,025	90	90	81	90	90	90	90	64	72	72	98	98
15		Housing	2,400	200	200	200	200	200	200	200	200	200	200	200	200
16		Cell Phone	480	40	40	40	40	40	40	40	40	40	40	40	40
17		Cable & Internet	360	30	30	30	30	30	30	30	30	30	30	30	30
18		Auto Maint'nce	600	50	50	50	50	50	50	50	50	50	50	50	50
19		Auto Insurance	960	80	80	80	80	80	80	80	80	80	80	80	80
20		Groceries	960	80	80	80	80	80	80	80	80	80	80	80	80
21		Total Fixed Exp	6,785	570	570	561	570	570	570	570	544	552	552	578	578
22															
23		Variable													
24		Auto - Gas	670	50	50	50	50	50	50	60	70	70	70	50	50
25		Entertainment	680	50	70	50	50	50	50	50	70	70	70	50	50
26		Clothing	270		50	70			50		50			50	
27		Gifts	300	50	100			50			50		50		
28		Utilities:Elect'cty	450	30	40	50	50	50	40	30	20	40	50	20	30
29	10%	Contingency	925	78	89	79	73	78	77	72	81	74	80	75	71
30		Total Variable	3,295	256	399	299	223	278	267	212	341	254	320	245	201
31		Total Expenses	10,080	826	969	860	793	848	837	782	885	806	872	823	779
32															
33		Net Revenue	10,184	892	892	808	892	892	892	892	640	720	720	972	972
34		Less Expenses	10,080	826	969	860	793	848	837	782	885	806	872	823	779
35		Net Cash Flow	104	66	(77)	(52)	99	44	55	110	(245)	(86)	(152)	149	193
36		Net Flow %	1%	7%	-9%	-6%	11%	5%	6%	12%	-38%	-12%	-21%	15%	20%
37		Cumul Net Flow		66	(11)	(63)	36	80	135	245		(86)	(238)	(89)	104
38				Apr	May	Jun	Jul	Aug	Sep	Oct	Nov	Dec	Jan	Feb	Mar

FIGURE 10.3. Sample Budget

1. Row 1 shows you can start an annual budget any time of the year!
2. Track gross income in addition to the net income on a paycheck. This raises awareness to changing tax rules. See rows 2–10.
3. Cells A8 and A9 (where column A and rows 8–9 meet) contain the percentage of gross income that yields the net income. The percentage is calculated by dividing net income by gross income and multiplying by 100.
4. Expenses have two major categories: fixed and variable. Fixed expenses start on row 13; variable expenses start on row 23.
5. The savings amount (row 14) is treated like a fixed expense. "Pay yourself first!" Remember, *The Richest Man in Babylon* suggests 10 percent (cell A14), or you can "cheat" and use 11 percent or more. (See idea 10-4 for more on starting on the path to saving money.)
6. The categories "Auto Maintenance" and "Auto Insurance" (rows 18–19) show how to budget an expense that you incur only a few times a year. Auto insurance (row 19) typically is a semiannual payment. In the example (row 19), the annual payment is $960, so the semiannual payment

is $480. To prevent the "I don't have the money when the semiannual bill is due" problem, budget $480 ÷ 6 = $80 a month. Put that money away monthly in a different savings account from the Arkad account. When the bill is due, you'll have the money and will have earned a little interest.

7. Auto maintenance (row 18) is similar. You know you'll have auto maintenance expenses at some point, so estimate them and put money aside monthly. You'll have it when it's time to do maintenance on your car.

8. The gas expense (row 24) varies based on work, play, and vacation activities.

9. Expenses like electricity (row 28) typically change from season to season.

10. Row 29 is the budget for unexpected expenses like a flat tire, often called "contingency." Cell A29 shows a 10 percent contingency, a common number to use. The 10 percent is calculated on the sum of all fixed expenses and all variable expenses above the contingency line. If you have only some or no contingency expenses in a given month, deposit the remaining contingency funds into your Arkad account.

11. "The Bottom Line." What is your cash flow? "Cash flow" is the flow of money in and out of accounts. It can be positive or negative. Positive means a surplus; negative means a deficit. Rows 33 and 34 are copies of the total net revenue (row 10) and total net expenses (row 31), respectively. The difference in row 35 (net revenue minus expenses) is the net cash flow for each month. (Note that cash flow is not the same as profit.)

12. Row 36 is the net flow percentage, which is calculated by taking net cash flow, dividing by net revenue, and multiplying by 100. This can be negative, meaning expenses exceeded revenue that month.

13. Row 37 is key: *cumulative* net cash flow takes into account the cash flow as it carries over from month to month. For example, the net cash flow entering June (cell F35) is ($52), yielding a cumulative net cash flow of ($63) for June (cell F37). With a cash flow of $99 in July (cell G35), the cumulative net cash flow in July is ($63) + $99 = $36 (cell G37). August's net cash flow adds $44 (cell H35) to the cumulative net cash flow, which then stands at $80 (cell H37). (Reminder: a number in parentheses denotes a negative number.)

* Takeaway   Keeping a budget helps increase savings and control expenses.

* Take action!   Start a budget *now*. See idea 10-11 for bud-
                                        geting resources.

10-13. LEARN ECONOMICS IN ONE SHORT LESSON

How do you make sense of the myriad of economic perspectives that are
presented daily online, in the press, in books, or wherever? Here's a simple
approach.

Andrew J. Galambos taught about Henry Hazlitt, who wrote a classic book,
Economics in One Lesson, first published in 1946. It reads as if it was written
yesterday, starting with the opening sentence of chapter 1: "Economics is
haunted by more fallacies than any other subject known to man."

A mere two pages later comes his one economics lesson:

The art of economics consists in looking not merely at the immediate but at the
longer effects of any act or policy; it consists in tracing the consequences of that
policy not merely for one group but for all groups.

Sidebar: This lesson can also be applied to the art of parenting, relationships, teamwork, and so much more.

In the section "The Lesson Applied," Mr. Hazlitt uses a simple example to
demonstrate the fallacies of most economic policies. His story of "The Broken
Window" tells of a baker in a small town whose shop window is broken when
someone heaves a brick through it. The baker contacts the glazier and pays
$50 (in 1946!) for a new window. The townspeople point out a "positive" side:
if the window had not been broken, the glazier would not have had the $50,
which he can now spend with other merchants. So the hoodlum appears to be
a public benefactor, "creating" new business.

But *unknown to everyone*, the baker had planned to buy a new suit for $50
(in 1946!) that day, but he now cannot afford it. *The townspeople don't know*
about the tailor! The $50 that would have gone to the tailor now goes to the
glazier. No *new* employment has been created. People will never see the new
suit because it will not be created.

Mr. Hazlitt closes the story with a comment on the townspeople: "They see
only what is immediately visible to the eye."

This broken-window fallacy is one of many in the book. The point: there
is *nothing* in existing economic policies (which are fallacies for the most part)

that can predict economic outcomes with any reasonable degree of certainty. There are too many unknowns involved in predicting human behavior and global commerce flow for that to happen. Yet many governments and private companies project economic activity and present it to the people as if they can make it happen.

"A politician needs the ability to foretell what is going to happen tomorrow, next week, next month, and next year. And to have the ability afterwards to explain why it didn't happen."

—Winston Churchill (1874–1965)

The baker/glazier/tailor story is an example of the law of unintended consequences. Wikipedia explains the law as "an adage or idiomatic warning that an intervention in a complex system tends to create unanticipated and often undesirable outcomes." See http://en.wikipedia.org/wiki/Unintended_consequences.

Here's a current example (regardless of when you read this book): when a sports team goes to a championship—think Super Bowl, World Series, NCAA Final Four, and such—people spend money on team-related merchandise, and they travel to and stay in hotels in the city where the competition is held. They spend impressive sums of money on tickets, team clothing, restaurants, and other fun.

But what about where that money might otherwise have been spent or saved? Other businesses, investment accounts, charities, and the like will never know what money might have passed their way. The message is *not*, "Therefore, don't do it." The message is that when a city reports a windfall of $30 million, $50 million, or $100 million, it *automatically* means that those are sums of money that were not spent or saved elsewhere.

Think of the suit the baker didn't buy.

The broken-window fallacy is an example of not tracing all the consequences of economic activity for all groups. The Great Law of the Iroquois is to look at consequences of proposed major changes "unto the seventh generation."

The short version of this economics lesson is this:

"When we try to pick out something by itself, we find it hitched to
everything else in the universe."

—*John Muir (1838–1914)*

| * Takeaway | It is extremely difficult to state with accuracy the outcome of economic policies and predictions. |
| * Take Action! | Read the first few pages of Henry Hazlitt's *Economics in One Lesson*, at least through "The Broken Window." |

10-14. CASH AND CREDIT CARD MANAGEMENT

How can you manage your cash and credit cards? (For the latter, the easiest
way is not to use them.) The software product Quicken, by Intuit, is one of the
best software products ever written. It has grown from a simple checkbook-
register manager to include a suite of features:

1. Budgeting and planning
2. Downloading your bank account transactions directly into Quicken for reconciliation
3. Credit card tracking and management
4. Investing
5. Mobile phone apps
6. Online bill paying and automatic reconciliation
7. Reports and graphs (dozens of them, sorted by category, date, payee, etc.)
8. Checkbook register

For more information, visit www.intuit.com. Intuit also sells another outstanding product designed for small businesses, QuickBooks. Another service
for cash management from Intuit is www.mint.com, which has no additional
cost.

| * Takeaway | Consider using a software product or app to manage your budget. |
| * Take Action! | See item 116 for budgeting 10-11. |

10-15. YOUR CREDIT REPORT AND CREDIT SCORE

Know what's in your credit report! By law, you can get annual credit reports from the three credit-reporting agencies (www.Equifax.com, www.Experian .com, and www.Transunion.com) at no additional cost at the website www .AnnualCreditReport.com. Check the reports thoroughly for names you've never used (like "null"), addresses you've never lived at, and phone numbers you've never had. The three credit agencies have online or written services to dispute and correct credit reports. Your credit score is available anytime at no additional cost from www.CreditKarma.com.

10-16. COMMON MISTAKES ABOUT WEALTH, FINANCES, AND INVESTING

Common mistakes center on the following:

1. Not following the ideas of *The Richest Man in Babylon*, especially saving regularly.
2. Spending money without a budget.
3. Relying on "experts" and not yourself to save your money.

TAKEAWAY SUMMARY

10-1. You get to decide what wealth means to you.

10-2. There are very few "needs"; most things are "wants," which are choices.

10-3. *You* decide (choose) your worth.

10-4. It's tough to start building wealth until you start saving money.

10-5. Small savings here and there accumulate into large ones.

10-6. There are methodical ways of getting out of debt.

10-7. Establish credit with one or more secure credit cards.

10-8. Time is on your side with the power of compound interest.

10-9. Growing money with compound interest means you have the money later, even if it's worth less.

10-10. Keeping a budget helps increase savings and control expenses.

10-11. Consider using a software product or app to manage your budget.

10-12. Keeping a budget helps increase savings and control expenses.

10-13. It is extremely difficult to state with accuracy the outcome of economic policies and predictions.

10-14. Consider using a software product or app to manage your budget.

Thinking of Your Own Small Business?

"Seventy percent of small businesses are owned and operated by a single person."

—Source: *https://www.buzzfeednews.com/article/jessicamisener/*

The main ideas to consider while running a business are how to do the following:

- Name and brand your company.
- Acquire basic business skills.
- Focus on a niche product or service.
- Understand profit and its use.
- Apply proven business techniques, such as how or why to:
    a. Ask useful questions to close a sale.
    b. Help customers become self-sufficient.
    c. Eliminate time wasters.
    d. Use written contracts.
    e. Model your business.
- Apply principles from a custom-software service business to:
    a. Pay staff.
    b. Work as a team with customers.
    c. Develop fixed-price quotes.

11-1. THINKING OF STARTING YOUR OWN SMALL BUSINESS?

"Business is a matter of human service."

—Milton Hershey (1857–1945)
(Yes, as in Hershey chocolates.)

There's a saying, "When you work for yourself, you only work half-time. You get to pick which twelve hours!"

The first few sections in this chapter offer ideas and considerations on starting your own small business. Sections after that have more detailed ideas to consider. An important consideration is that you need to understand clearly *why* you want to have your own business. Your understanding and firm beliefs will be the propulsion that powers you through the uncertain times that will almost certainly follow.

Here are some of the reasons people start their own small businesses:

1. Produce better products or services than other companies or individuals.
2. Produce unique or niche-market products or services.
3. Have a greater degree of time flexibility compared with working for someone else.
4. Have more family time, especially with businesses run from the home.
5. Make money doing something they love.
6. Work alone.
7. Create jobs.
8. Make the world a better place by improving the lives of their customers.

* Takeaway	If you're passionate about a skill you have and do it well, you have the basis of creating a business to harness that passion.
* Take Action!	Do a "Ben Franklin" (idea 7-19) on starting your own business vs. whatever else you're doing now.

Note: There are only four more "Take Action!" suggestions in this chapter. If you want to start your own business, you'll have your own "Take Action!" to-do list. ☺

11-2. NAMING AND BRANDING YOUR COMPANY

Choose a name that reinforces your brand and conjures a favorable image in people's minds. There are consultants who charge six- and seven-figure amounts to help companies come up with names and brand names, but we'll use our own brains. Ever hear of a company named "Apple" and its product "Macintosh"? How about "the "Cheesecake Factory"? The name should be easy to pronounce and spell, because you want people to be able to find you easily. Stay away from "cutesy pie," long names, and odd spellings like "Kozy Kwilts." People will have trouble finding you. Though a name like Organized Information Corporation gives a slight hint of what the company does, it is a mouthful to say and remember.

If you're thinking of a service business, consider a name that includes yours to reinforce your brand. Something as simple as "John Doe's Painting" says who you are and what you do! Stay away from names that are location or address dependent as street names sometimes do change. Besides, you want to reinforce your brand name, not the location's name.

* Takeaway	Consider a company name carefully. Use words that create simple, positive images in people's minds.

11-3. ACQUIRE BUSINESS SKILLS

Many small-business entrepreneurs are notoriously poor business*people*. Often they are too excited about selling their products or services to do such mundane tasks as balancing a checkbook or paying bills and taxes on time. Acquire basic business skills and budget time in your workweek to handle the administrative part. Don't go through life thinking Accounts Payable entries are what companies have to pay you. If you still think that, search www.night ingale.com for "business skills" to find material to get you started.

If you truly dislike managing a business, hire out some of the administrative tasks like bookkeeping and accounting. Intuit's QuickBooks is an easy-to-use software package that tracks business tasks like checkbook management, time management, invoicing, and budgeting.

11-4. FOCUS: WHAT IS YOUR NICHE?

One of the harder parts of running a business is the temptation to be all things to all customers. Huge corporations may have the personnel and financial resources to do so, but a small business does not. Identify your niche, develop it, and stick to it, at least as you are getting started.

For example, in an attempt to create a "one-stop shopping" environment for their customers, software companies sometimes try to provide hardware, too. But their expertise is in software, not hardware, so who is going to support the hardware when it needs servicing? Won't that take away from the focus on software, their strength? Answer: yes.

11-5. TEAMWORK

If you're a lousy administrator, team up with someone who's good at it and enjoys it. If you're a lousy salesperson, team up with someone who's good at it and enjoys it. If you don't like doing certain aspects of running a business, find someone who likes running a business and is good at it. Note the theme: "and is good at it." You might be tempted to ask friends and relatives to help, but are they good at what you're asking them to do?

* Takeaway

Teamwork enables you to accomplish a lot more than only what you're good at. Work with people who shore up your weaknesses. (If you have none, publish how you did it.)

11-6. PROFIT: WHAT IT IS AND WHAT IT'S FOR

Is profit good or bad?

One definition. The Oxford English Dictionary defines profit as "a financial gain, esp. the difference between the amount earned and the amount spent in buying, operating, or producing something." (For another discussion of profit, see idea 9-10.)

Profit fuels business expansions like upgrading or adding computers, attending business-related seminars, offering health care to employees, or running a new marketing campaign. Plain and simple.

* Takeaway   Profit is necessary to grow a business.

11-7. CORPORATION, SOLE PROPRIETORSHIP, LLC, OR DBA?

Should you form a corporation, sole proprietorship, limited liability corporation (LLC), or "doing business as" (DBA)? There are *many* tax implications to your decision, so research what works best for you. Consult with an
accountant and tax attorney to understand the implications. This is not a
recommendation, but the easiest, lowest-cost approach is to use a DBA. You
register your business name on your state's Secretary of State website. The
fee for creating a DBA is usually under $100, and the DBA generally has to
be renewed annually for a nominal fee. Securing a DBA enables you to open
business checking and savings accounts to keep your business transactions
separate from your personal transactions, which is essential for IRS filing
and reporting. Note that a DBA does not provide the legal protection that a
corporation does.

11-8. ASSORTED GENERAL IDEAS THAT (EVENTUALLY) WORKED

The next few sections describe general ideas that, after many mistakes along
the way, ended up working well for a small business providing services (as
opposed to one selling products). Following these sections is a separate set
of ideas that originated in a custom-software business but can apply to any
service business.

An outstanding resource for service companies is the book *Selling the
Invisible*, by Harry Beckwith. Mr. Beckwith gives timeless advice on selling
intangible services ("invisible products," as he calls them).

* Takeaway	Learning to run a business involves trial and error and learning from failure.

Sales Strategies That Work

Businesses or people with problems are opportunities for service companies.
Here are two simple sales strategies that work well:

1. Find out what people want and give it to them.
2. Help people find out what they want.

To implement these two strategies, you need to know your customer. Ask questions and listen. Your customers will almost always tell you what they want, but you have to hear it to know it!

There are thousands of ideas on the web for closing sales. Find ones that work with your personality. (See www.nightingale.com for examples.) Be prepared to move out of your comfort zone and to hear "no" a lot. Attend sales seminars and try out new approaches. And also be prepared to hear "no" a lot. ☺

Sidebar: An excellent sales-support resource is the website www.salesforce.com. It has contact management, proposal tracking, sales tracking, and a whole lot more. It is a low-cost way to get started.

* Takeaway
There are thousands of sales techniques. Locate people or strategies successful at sales and learn from them.

Help Customers Become Self-Sufficient

Sometimes prospects are hesitant to get involved with a service company for fear of becoming too dependent on them and spending too much money. To assuage their fears, tell them, "We'll work our way out of the job so you can take care of yourselves." If customers perceive that you are truly there to help them become self-sufficient, they will view you as an extension of themselves and want to do business with you.

* Takeaway
Help customers become self-sufficient.

Short, Crisp Proposals

While stereotypical salespeople are known for rah-rah performances, most people are not comfortable with that. A more proactive sales approach that respects people's time and money is to write proposals with an Executive Summary on page 1 that lists *all* the crucial information a businessperson requires to make a decision: investment amount, schedule, resources needed, payment plan, and so on. The rest of the proposal should back up the numbers on page 1. Don't bury important details on page 22. People appreciate this format's openness.

Also write proposals from the perspective of "Why would they buy from us *again*?" That helps you bring to the surface many win-win situations that build trust.

    * Takeaway   Write proposals that are clear, concise, and correct.

Eliminate Time Wasters

A great time-respecting perspective is this:

"What gets measured gets done."

—Andrew Grove (1936–2016), Intel employee #3

First, estimate how long tasks will take and follow up by recording (measuring) how much time they took. Estimating skills can be developed primarily by trial and error. This may sound simplistic, but if a project is estimated at ten thousand hours and $1 million, it's important to know how much time and money has been expended so you can know how far along a project is. You'd be surprised at how many projects fail mostly because of poor time and funds management.

In a meeting with, say, ten people, be aware that a minute wasted means a minute wasted for ten people, or a total of ten minutes wasted. This awareness helps you contribute to maintaining focus during a meeting.

Ways to eliminate time wasters:

1. Use a to-do list that you rewrite and prioritize every evening.
2. For a few days, write down in quarter-hour increments how you spend your time. You'll be amazed at how much wasted time you'll find—time when you could be doing something else. Also, you'll probably be more conscious of how you are using your time while you're measuring it.
3. Handle each piece of paper or e-mail once. One project-management outcome from the Apollo space project—there had never been a project like it before in history—was the concept of "dump, delay, do, or delegate."
   a. Dump: Don't do the task! It could be busywork in disguise, like arranging your paper clips by color.
   b. Delay: Do the task later, but schedule now a time to do it.
   c. Do: Do the task and get it done.

d. Delegate: Give someone else the opportunity to complete the task.

4. "Do it once right." There always seems to be time for do-overs, but it's more economical in time and money to do things right the first time.

| * Takeaway | Know how and where you use your time so you can guard it well. |

The Purpose of a Written Contract

Verbal agreements are not binding in court—hence the written contract. Its main purposes are to:

1. spell out the products or services to be delivered;
2. establish the investment and schedule;
3. designate who is responsible for what;
4. indicate what to do if there is a dispute; and
5. cover contingencies.

Then, proceed on trust. If you are concerned about trusting a potential customer, don't enter into the contract. An untrustworthy person will find ways out of it. Here is a paragraph from a service contract that shows one example of covering contingencies, but be sure to get legal advice before incorporating any of these ideas into a contract.

> Arbitration. Should Client and Contractor enter into a dispute which they cannot resolve together, they agree to submit the dispute to binding arbitration subject to the rules of the American Arbitration Association. Client and Contractor will each select an arbitrator, and those two arbitrators will select a third arbitrator who will hear and rule on the dispute.

THIS IS NOT A RECOMMENDATION TO USE THIS PARAGRAPH. It merely illustrates one approach to conflict resolution in a business relationship.

| * Takeaway | Written, not verbal, agreements are sound approaches to define all aspects of a project with a prospect or customer. |

Business Modeling

If you're thinking of starting a business, consider modeling its projected performance. A business model is a spreadsheet that shows income and expenses projected forward anywhere from six months to five years. Entrepreneurs approaching venture capitalists typically prepare a five-year business model as part of their presentation package. Or, if you're planning a small business to run from your home, you might project six months to two years ahead.

Figure 11.1 is a model of a small service business whose primary source of income and expenses is labor. To simplify the model, we use two levels of technical staff—project leaders (PL) and programmer/analysts (PA)—and one administrator (AD). The principles apply to companies selling products, too.

				4.1					Effective April			
Line	Work Hrs/Month:	164	40	Base			Billing	Benefits	New		Income	Expenses
			# on	Hourly	Hourly		Rate	Hourly	Hourly		$590,400	$488,466
	Staff	Id	Staff	Month	Pay Rate	Markup %	o Custome	Cost %	Cost %			
	Project Leader	PL	2	164	$60.00	100%	$120.00	20%	23%			
	Programmer	PA	6	164	$30.00	100%	$60.00	20%	22%			
	Administrator	AD	1	164	$14.25		$14.25	20%	22%			
	INCOME	Staff		January	February	March	April	May	June	Total		
	Hours	PL		328	328	328	328	328	328	1,968		
	Pay Rate/Hour			$60.00	$60.00	$60.00	$60.00	$60.00	$60.00			
	Billing Rate/Hour			$120.00	$120.00	$120.00	$120.00	$120.00	$120.00			
A	Total Income PL			$39,360	$39,360	$39,360	$39,360	$39,360	$39,360	$236,160	40.0%	
	Hours	PA		984	984	984	984	984	984	5,904		
	Pay Rate/Hour		$30.00	$30.00	$30.00	$30.00	$30.00	$30.00	$30.00			
	Billing Rate/Hour		$60.00	$60.00	$60.00	$60.00	$60.00	$60.00	$60.00			
B	Total Income PA			$59,040	$59,040	$59,040	$59,040	$59,040	$59,040	$354,240	60.0%	
	Total Income PL + PA			$98,400	$98,400	$98,400	$98,400	$98,400	$98,400	$590,400	100.0%	
	DIRECT LABOR COSTS											
	Benefits Cost %	PL		20%	20%	20%	23%	23%	23%			
	Total Cost/Hour			$72.00	$72.00	$72.00	$73.80	$73.80	$73.80			
C	Total Labor Cost			$23,616	$23,616	$23,616	$24,206	$24,206	$24,206	$143,467	24.3%	29.4%
	Gross Profit/Hour			$48.00	$48.00	$48.00	$46.20	$46.20	$46.20			
	Gross Profit			$15,744	$15,744	$15,744	$15,154	$15,154	$15,154	$92,693	15.7%	19.0%
	Gross Profit %			40%	40%	40%	39%	39%	39%			

FIGURE 11.1. Sample Business Model (1 of 3)

	Benefits Cost %	PA	20%	20%	20%	20%	22%	22%	22%			
	Total Cost/Hour			$36.00	$36.00	$36.00	$36.60	$36.60				
D	Total Labor Cost			$35,424	$35,424	$35,424	$36,014	$36,014	$36,014	$214,315	36.3%	43.9%
	Gross Profit/Hour			$24.00	$24.00	$24.00	$23.40	$23.40				
	Gross Profit			$23,616	$23,616	$23,616	$23,026	$23,026	$23,026	$139,925	23.7%	28.6%
	Gross Profit %			40%	40%	40%	39%	39%	39%			
	Hours	AD		164	164	164	164	164	164	984		
	Pay Rate/Hour			$14.25	$14.25	$14.25	$14.25	$14.25	$14.25			
	Benefits Cost %			20%	20%	20%	22%	22%	22%			
	Total Cost/Hour			$17.10	$17.10	$17.10	$17.39	$17.39	$17.39			
E	Total Labor Cost			$2,804	$2,804	$2,804	$2,852	$2,852	$2,852	$16,969	2.9%	3.5%
F	Totals for	Sales		$98,400	$98,400	$98,400	$98,400	$98,400	$98,400	$590,400		
G	PL + PA + AD	Cost		$61,844	$61,844	$61,844	$63,073	$63,073	$63,073	$374,751		
H		Gross Profit		$36,556	$36,556	$36,556	$35,327	$35,327	$35,327	$215,649		
		Gross Profit %		37%	37%	37%	36%	36%	36%	37%		
K	Savings		11%	$10,820	$10,820	$10,820	$10,820	$10,820	$10,820	$64,520	11.0%	13.3%
	OTHER EXPENSES											
	Insurance - Liability		$75	$75	$75	$75	$75	$75	$75	$450	0.08%	0.09%
	Insurance - Renter		$25	$25	$25	$25	$25	$25	$25	$150	0.03%	0.03%
	Office Supplies		$70	$70	$70	$70	$70	$70	$70	$420	0.07%	0.09%
	Phone - Cell		$100	$100	$100	$100	$100	$100	$100	$600	0.10%	0.12%

FIGURE 11.1. Sample Business Model (2 of 3)

	A	B	D	E	F	G	H	I	J	K	L	M
59		Staff Training	$600	$600	$600	$600	$600	$600	$600	$3,600	0.61%	0.74%
60		Travel & Entertainment	$300	$300	$300	$300	$300	$300	$300	$1,800	0.30%	0.37%
61		Utilities	$100	$100	$100	$100	$100	$100	$100	$600	0.10%	0.12%
62	L	Subtotal Other Expenses		$3,895	$3,895	$3,895	$3,895	$3,895	$3,895	$23,370	3.96%	4.78%
63		Contingency for the Above	10%	$390	$390	$390	$390	$390	$390	$2,340	0.40%	0.48%
64		Taxes - FICA - Medicare	1.45%	$1,427	$1,427	$1,427	$1,427	$1,427	$1,427	$8,562	1.45%	1.75%
65		Taxes - FICA - SocSec	6.20%	$6,101	$6,101	$6,101	$6,101	$6,101	$6,101	$36,606	6.20%	7.49%
66		Taxes - Unemployment	1.50%	$1,476	$1,476	$1,476	$1,476	$1,476	$1,476	$8,856	1.50%	1.81%
67	M	Total Other Expenses		$13,289	$13,289	$13,289	$13,289	$13,289	$13,289	$79,734	13.51%	16.32%
68												
69	[F]	Total Sales		$98,400	$98,400	$98,400	$98,400	$98,400	$98,400	$590,400	100.0%	
70	N	Total Labor+Other Expenses		$75,133	$75,133	$75,133	$76,362	$76,362	$76,362	$454,485	77.0%	93.0%
71	P	Pre-Tax Profit (Loss)		$23,267	$23,267	$23,267	$22,038	$22,038	$22,038	$135,915	23.0%	27.8%
72		Pre-Tax Profit (Loss) %		23.6%	23.6%	23.6%	22.4%	22.4%	22.4%	23.0%		
73												
74		Taxes - Federal	15.00%	$3,490	$3,490	$3,490	$3,306	$3,306	$3,306	$20,388	3.5%	4.2%
75		Taxes - State	10.00%	$2,327	$2,327	$2,327	$2,204	$2,204	$2,204	$13,593	2.3%	2.8%
76	Q	Total Income Tax		$5,817	$5,817	$5,817	$5,510	$5,510	$5,510	$33,981	5.8%	7.0%
77	R	Total All Expenses		$80,950	$80,950	$80,950	$81,872	$81,872	$81,872	$488,466	82.7%	100.0%

FIGURE 11.1. Sample Business Model (3 of 3)

* Takeaway — Modeling a business gives glimpses at its viability.

* Take Action! — Create a sample business model and study its revenue and expense projections.

Sales Projections

Sales projections are typically fluid spreadsheets that can change daily, weekly, or monthly, depending on your type of business. A short-term (two- to five-week) projection helps you determine how to allocate your time among closing sales, writing new proposals, and doing the work the customer hired you for. This is invaluable in setting priorities.

Figure 11.2 contains a sample sales and expense projection.

	A	B	C	D	E	G	H	I
1		Projected New Revenue from Modernizing a Website						Weeks/Month
2	Line	Cells backlit in blue: assumptions	Weekly Estimates			Monthly Estimates		4.1
3	1	INTERNET TRAFFIC	Low	Medium	High	Low	Medium	High
4	2	# of online visitors (from Analytics)	1,000	1,000	1,000	4,100	4,100	4,100
5	3	% who become customers	2%	4%	6%			
6	4	Net # of new customers	20	40	60	82	164	246
7	5	% who refer other business	5%	10%	15%			
8	6	Net # of referred customers	1	4	9	4	16	37
9	7	Total # of new customers	21	44	69	86	180	283
10	8	Average sale/new customer	$ 100	$ 200	$ 300			
11	9	Projected sales from ONLINE	$ 2,100	$ 8,800	$ 20,700	$ 8,610	$ 36,080	$ 84,870
12	10							
13	11	MOBILE DEVICE TRAFFIC						
14	12	# of mobile visitors (from Analytics)	100	100	100	410	410	410
15	13	% who become customers	4%	8%	12%			
16	14	Net # of new customers	4	8	12	16	33	49
17	15	% who refer other business	8%	12%	20%			
18	16	Net # of referred customers	0	0	2	0	0	8
19	17	Total # of new customers	4	8	14	16	33	57
20	18	Average sale/new customer	$ 200	$ 350	$ 500			
21	19	Projected sales from MOBILE	$ 800	$ 2,800	$ 7,000	$ 3,280	$ 11,480	$ 28,700
22	20							

FIGURE 11.2. Sample Sales Projection (1 of 2)

	A	B	C	D	E	F	G	H	I
23	21	Total INTERNET + MOBILE							
24	22	Gross # of visitors	1,100	1,100	1,100	4,510	4,510	4,510	
25	23	Visitors who become customers	24	48	72	98	197	295	
26	24	% who become customers	2.2%	4.4%	6.5%	2.2%	4.4%	6.5%	
27	25	Net # of referred customers	1	4	11	4	16	45	
28	26	Total # of new customers	25	52	83	103	213	340	
29	27	Net % of visitors who become customers	2.3%	4.7%	7.5%	2.3%	4.7%	7.5%	
30	28	Projected total sales	$ 2,900	$ 11,600	$ 27,700	$ 11,890	$ 47,560	$ 113,570	
31	29	Average sale/new customer	$ 116	$ 223	$ 333	$ 116	$ 223	$ 333	
32	30	ADDITIONAL 12-MONTH REVENUE	$142,680	$ 570,720	$ 1,362,840	$142,680	$ 570,720	$ 1,362,840	
33									
34	Notes								
35									
36	1.	Numbers backlit are assumptions. All other cells are calculated.							
37	2.	This estimate assumes current Web traffic. The traffic would increase with more advertising.							
38	3.	Projections do not include revenues from the new customers who give repeat business.							

FIGURE 11.2. Sample Sales Projection (2 of 2)

* Takeaway	Sales and expense projections help determine priorities and goals.
* Take Action!	Create a sales and expense projection.

Maintaining Contact with Prospects and Customers

To maintain contact with prospects and customers, here are a few guidelines.

Whenever feasible, use the human touch and call or visit. Don't e-mail or text! Having a conversation with someone makes it a lot easier to find out information than through e-mail or texting. Besides, if you are *truly* interested in your customers as people, you'll want to have a conversation anyway. If you have a web-based national or international business, visiting customers is not viable, but you certainly can make phone calls to give and receive personal perspectives.

If you tell a customer you'll call on Tuesday at two o'clock with a status report, call on Tuesday at two o'clock with a status report. The report might be that there is no new status, but make the call anyway.

"Trust takes years to build and seconds to lose."

—*Anonymous*

Following Up on Sales Proposals

Based on statistics from the world of sales, the average sale is closed on the fifth sales call, but the average salesperson makes only two sales calls to a prospect about a proposal. Do the math. Make five, six, seven calls—or as many as necessary to make the sale.

After closing a sale, handwrite a thank-you note to your customer for the business and the beginning of a long-term relationship. Few people get handwritten notes these days, so yours will stand out. Address the envelope in writing and write "Personal" to the left of the address. This significantly adds to the likelihood that your note will be opened. Also, the next time you meet, ask your new customer for referrals.

After losing a sale, handwrite a thank-you note to the prospect for considering your proposal. You never know whether the chosen vendor will work out, and if not, you're available to pick up the project.

When getting in touch with customers and prospects—say, to follow up on a submitted proposal—keep in mind that your urgency is not theirs. Meeting your payroll is not their problem. A great tool for keeping in touch with customers and tracking sales and project activity is the website www.salesforce.com.

* Takeaway	Maintain contact with customers and prospects using personal approaches.

Luck in Business

Does luck play a role in business? You bet, as it does anywhere in life. Luck happens to those who have feelers "out there" in the marketplace.

"The more I practice, the luckier I get."

—*Ben Hogan (1912–1997), professional golfer*

---

* Takeaway	Luck is what happens when you keep pushing forward!

Quality vs. Price

Here is a tongue-in-cheek view of pricing a product:

* Meets requirements
* Good quality
* Cheap price
Pick any two!

| * Takeaway | Quality requires money and time. |

"Each Word Costs $1"

To learn to write concisely, imagine each word you write costs $1 (or $10 or $100) in profit. This leads to a mental game, "How can I keep costs down when writing proposals or documents for my customers and prospects?" This approach is a motivator to practice the three Cs: writing that is clear, concise, and correct.

| * Takeaway | "Vigorous writing is concise." |
| | —*Strunk and White in* The Elements of Style |

11-9. ASSORTED CUSTOM-PROGRAMMING BUSINESS IDEAS THAT (EVENTUALLY) WORKED

Even if you have or are considering a different kind of business, these ideas might be useful.

Bring Two Copies of Anything You Install

If you bring electronic files to a customer site for installation, bring *two* electronic copies with the files on two separate media like flash drives. If you bring just one copy of the software and the media is defective, you've wasted your customer's and your own time, and you've delayed any payment you might receive for a completed project or phase. Alternatively, have a backup copy in the Cloud, but be aware that the internet connection might be down.

One Way to Pay Programmers

There are three basic compensation guidelines for programmers:

1. Pay programmers the same hourly rate for all hours worked, except for item 3. That holds whether the hours per week are one, 168 (twenty-four times seven), or anything in between. There is no overtime, but people can work any number of hours a week and take vacation or personal time as often as they want as long as the work got done. (Confirm that your state has no laws against no overtime for programming professionals.)

2. A programmer's pay rate is half the hourly rate you charge a customer. (The other half pays for the cost of running the business, including the owner's salary.)
3. If there's a bug in a program, the programmer fixes it on his or her own time without compensation.

There are four major advantages to this approach:

1. Enable programmers to set their own schedules around family obligations and their own productive times of day.
2. Simplify a typically complicated compensation structure.
3. Create incentives for programmers to work productively and competently.
4. Create incentives for programmers to cultivate relationships with customers, which often lead to more projects.

* Takeaway	Consider your employee-compensation approach carefully so that it respects staff time and incentivizes competent work.

Codevelopment

Codevelopment works well in helping customers become self-sufficient and can be used in any labor-intensive business. The concept is simple: say you propose twenty hours for a certain task. Budget for the customer to perform some or all of the task—their time permitting—thereby saving them money. This approach also keeps customers actively engaged in the project, starts their training on using the system, and helps them learn what you are doing. These are all important steps toward self-sufficiency.

Figure 11.3 has a sample codevelopment proposal. Prospects and customers appreciate the detail. This also leads to the à la carte approach: a customer could decide simply not to implement a report or a screen as long as the underlying infrastructure isn't affected.

	A	B	C	D	E	F	G	H	I	
1			CoDevelopment Example for Implementation							
2										
3		This example shows customer participation in creating one of the screens and both reports.								
4										
5		PL Rate/Hour:	$80.00		PA Rate/Hour:	$40.00				
6										
7			Estimate			CoDevelopement Savings			Net	
8	Line	Sample Component	PL Hours	PA Hours	Extension	PL Hours	PA Hours	Savings	Investment	
9	1	Create System Infrastructure	3	2	$320				$320	
10	2	Implement Database Design	2	8	$480				$480	
11	3	Data Entry Screens	2		$160				$160	
12	4	Order Entry		6	$240		3	$120	$120	
13	5	Management Override		3	$120				$120	
14	6	Reports	2		$160				$160	
15	7	Orders (3 sorts)		4	$160		4	$160		
16	8	Backorders (3 sorts)		3	$120		3	$120		
17	9									
18	10	Totals:	9	26	$1,760		10	$400	$1,360	
19										
20							% Savings:	29.4%		

FIGURE 11.3. Codevelopment Example

* Takeaway   With codevelopment, involve customers in projects as much as they want to be involved.

Requirements Analysis First, Then a Fixed-Price Quote

Customers typically prefer a fixed-price quote over a time-and-materials quote (in which payment is by the hour). The main reason is that they can budget for the project more easily with a fixed-price quote because there is an upper limit to their costs.

However, one danger in quoting fixed-price software is that the requirements of the business might not be fully known. (In fact, most of the time requirements are *never* fully predictable because the business or the marketplace changes.) For example, until people see how a data-viewing screen looks, it is hard for them to imagine how it will work on a day-to-day basis. So break down projects into two phases:

1. Customers pay time and materials to work together with you to develop the requirements.
2. You then present a fixed-price quote for the design and implementation of the application. Changes to the requirements are quoted separately.

* Takeaway   The hardest aspect of creating software products (and tangible products, too) is knowing what the customer wants.

11-10. IF YOU WANT TO RAISE YOUR RATES

If you want to raise your rates, give your customers a few weeks' or months' notice and indicate what the new rates will be. Customers appreciate the warning and might even sign up for projects that have not been approved yet so they can take advantage of the lower rates.

11-11. COMMON MISTAKES IN STARTING AND RUNNING A BUSINESS

You will run into problems if you:

1. Don't learn about business basics before starting a business.
2. Ignore the ideas in *The Richest Man in Babylon* for the business. (See idea 10-4.)
3. Treat the financial aspect of running a business casually.
4. Don't realize the importance of human interaction over technical superiority. People have to feel comfortable before they buy.
5. Don't understand the role of corporate politics in customer decision making. A superior technical solution is not enough.
6. Keep certain staff members too long when they should be fired.
7. Have staff work without defining their goals.
8. Don't advertise and market well. In most cases, people do not beat a path (or e-path) to your door!
9. Don't plan for growth.

TAKEAWAY SUMMARY

11-1. If you're passionate about a skill you have and do it well, you have the basis of creating a business to harness that passion.

11-2. Consider a company name carefully. Use words that create simple, positive images in people's minds.

11-5. Teamwork enables you to accomplish a lot more than only what you're good at. Work with people who shore up your weaknesses. (If you have none, publish how you did it.)

11-6. Profit is necessary to grow a business.

11-8. Learning to run a business involves trial and error and learning from failure.

11-8. There are thousands of sales techniques. Locate people or strategies successful at sales and learn from them.

11-8. Help customers become self-sufficient.

11-8. Write proposals that are clear, concise, and correct.

11-8. Know how and where you use your time so you can guard it well.

11-8. Written, not verbal, agreements are sound approaches to define all aspects of a project with a prospect or customer.

11-8. Modeling a business gives glimpses at its viability.

11-8. Sales and expense projections help determine priorities and goals.

11-8. Maintain contact with customers and prospects using personal approaches.

11-8. Luck is what happens when you keep pushing forward!

11-8. Quality requires money and time.

11-8. "Vigorous writing is concise."

11-9. Consider your employee-compensation approach carefully so that it respects staff time and incentivizes competent work.

11-9. With codevelopment, involve customers in projects as much as they want to be involved.

11-9. The hardest aspect of creating software products (and tangible products, too) is knowing what the customer wants.

12

Dealing with a Mental Illness

"Bipolar disorder affects approximately 5.7 million adult Americans, or about 2.6% of the U.S. population age 18 and older every year."

—Source: *National Institute of Mental Health (2019)*

This chapter is included because there is a 25 percent chance that you or someone you know has a mental illness. If you don't, there is a high likelihood you will encounter someone with a mental illness or someone who knows another person(s) with one. Understanding some of the underlying concepts helps you deal with mental illness in the workplace and in private.

12-1. ABOUT MENTAL ILLNESSES

The National Alliance on Mental Illness defines a mental illness as "a medical condition that disrupts a person's thinking, feeling, mood, ability to relate to others, and daily functioning." Where does a mental illness end and the self begin? Is a mentally ill person equated with the illness? All mental illnesses are interwoven with their hosts' personalities and do not exist outside the mind. So a mental illness is merely *part* of a person, just like any other characteristic, such as height, weight, eye color, temperament, and intelligence.

Mental illness is not a shameful "act" or "history." It is a genetic aberration that, until the last few decades, people had no control over. Once diagnosed, people can make choices that determine whether they will obtain control.

Jason Hopcus makes a powerful point: we hear from the media about connections between mental illness and violence, but we don't often hear about the *millions* who successfully acknowledge their mental illnesses and lead happy, healthy, and balanced lives. This concept parallels how the media focus on one plane crash but do not report daily that tens of thousands of flights took off and landed without incident.

Though typically people see many improvements following treatment through medication, therapy, and habit adjustment, each person's *specific* response to treatment depends on his or her personality. The reference section has several resources for mental illnesses.

If you or someone you know suspect a mental illness, take care of it now before it seriously affects your life. Following are some tools for dealing with mental illness, using bipolar disorder (aka manic depression) as an example.

Mood Tracking

A common question after diagnosis is "How will I know if I'm getting better?" Tracking moods and feelings is a powerful tool. A few times a day, record moods and feelings by noting the time of day, a number from 0 to 10, and a brief comment on why you're feeling that way. A "0" represents deep depression (perhaps suicidal), "5" an even-keeled mood, and "10" runaway mania. There are two main purposes of tracking moods:

1. To establish a baseline for "normal" emotions
2. To learn how to recognize mood swings by thinking in terms of a numeric scale ("Oh, this feels like a 7")

Figure 12.1 shows part of a sample mood chart. It's followed by figure 12.2, a graph of the complete mood chart. To reduce the time needed to record entries, the sample chart uses twenty-four-hour time notation (14 means 2:00 p.m., for example). The December 5, 11:00 a.m. entry has the comment, "From a 1 to a 9 in one hour." From the graph, you can see why a nickname for bipolar disorder is "mood swing."

There are many mobile apps now for tracking and graphing moods.

Day	Hour	Mood	Comment
Dec 3	3	1	(Most comments have been removed for privacy)
	9	1	
	13	2	
	19	1	
Dec 4	4	1	
	7	3	
	9	1	
	17	3	
	22	1	
Dec 5	4	1	
	9	2	
	11	1	*From a "1" to a "9" in one hour*
	12	9	Feel like I could run 2 marathons then climb a mountain
	13	5	
	14	1	One hour before the appointment w/psychiatrist
	16	3	Leaving the psychiatrist's office after diagnosis
	18	4	Take first medication! Will it change things?
	22	4	
Dec 6	10	3	
	12	4	
	14	2	
	17	3	
	20	4	
Dec 7	18	4	
	21	6	
Dec 8	5	4	
	8	4	
	13	6	
	20	6	
	21	6	

FIGURE 12.1. Mood-Tracking Table

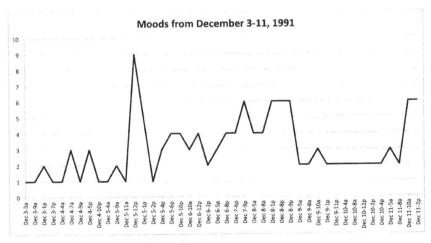

FIGURE 12.2. Mood-Tracking Chart

Sleep

For someone with bipolar disorder, lack of sleep can bring on mania.

Taking Medications

Some people with bipolar disorder don't take the recommended medications because they don't want to lose the indescribable highs that accompany mania. A big danger in not taking medication regularly, then resuming it, is that higher doses are needed to get back to the same level of therapeutic effectiveness. This, in turn, can lead to toxicity from the medication. To be effective, medications must be taken regularly.

Help from Family and Friends

Your family and friends believe in you. Though you are responsible for dealing with the illness, it is OK to lean on them for support.

In Case of Emergency

Keep a list of medications, dosages, and frequency in your wallet and in a metal case in your car's glove compartment. In case of an emergency in which you're incapacitated, someone will probably check your wallet or glove compartment for an ID and find the list there. Include other medical conditions, blood type, and your typical blood pressure in the list.

Dating

Amusing situations develop when it comes to dating and bipolar disorder. For example, *when* do you disclose your illness to someone you start seeing? If it's on the first date, there usually isn't a second one. If it's on the fifth or tenth date, the response is often, "Why didn't you tell me sooner?" ☺

A person who can see you for who you are *now* probably won't mind the illness. He or she might even recognize the truth that, for better or worse, bipolar disorder is part of what made you what you are now.

12-2. SIDEBAR: WHAT MAKES US HUMAN?

What makes us human? Mark Twain said, "Man is the only animal that blushes. Or needs to." How about cooking? We're the only species that cooks! Then there's compassion, empathy, creativity, reason, imagination, language, communication, self-talk, choice, planning, the capacity to learn (including learning from other people's mistakes!), the use of tools, and a whole lot more. With all the technology out there, let's remember the humanity aspect.

12-3. SIDEBAR: A CHALLENGE TO THE NEXT GENERATION

As a challenge to the next generation, answer a question about war that the previous generation didn't:

"How many deaths will it take 'til we know that too many people have died?"

—Bob Dylan (b. 1941), in the song "Blowin' in the Wind"

Unfortunately, war, too, is still a part of being human. If country leaders fought the wars they started instead of sending soldiers to die, war would end overnight.

13

Suggested Videos

Why these videos?

This chapter refers to a variety of videos available online. They are recommended because they offer tools for thinking for yourself, have great ideas to help prepare you for the real world, or are just plain fun. In each section, there's a summary of the video, its length (shown as mm:ss for minutes and seconds), and a link to it. All links worked as of the time this book was published.

13-1. EMOTIONAL INTELLIGENCE

Mr. Daniel Goleman gives a summary of his concept of Emotional Intelligence. (5:31)

https://www.youtube.com/watch?v=Y7m9eNoB3NU&app=desktop

13-2. STEVE JOBS—COMMENCEMENT ADDRESS AT STANFORD UNIVERSITY, 2005

Mr. Jobs presents three powerful ideas to the Stanford class of 2005 to consider as they enter the real world. (15:04)

http://www.youtube.com/watch?v=UF8uR6Z6KLc

13-3. SUSAN CAIN—THE POWER OF INTROVERTS

This TED video explains the power of introverts. The computer industry has a predominance of introverts, but introverts also abound in all walks of life. See idea 2-5 for more about introverts and extroverts. (19:05)

http://ed.ted.com/lessons/susan-cain-the-power-of-introverts

Also visit Ms. Cain's website, www.ThePowerOfIntroverts.com, and read her book titled *Quiet*. See www.ted.com for the world of TED videos.

13-4. DR. KELLY MCGONIGAL—HOW TO MAKE STRESS YOUR FRIEND

TED strikes again! Dr. Kelly McGonigal talks about how to make stress your friend. Stress is a normal occurrence in life; it's *how* you respond to it that makes a difference. See idea 7-8 for more on stress. (14:38)

http://www.ted.com/talks/kelly_mcgonigal_how_to_make_stress_your
_friend

13-5. OVERUSE OF MOBILE PHONES?

The two videos recommended in this section show the predominance of mobile devices in today's society. Let's remember the human interaction!

1. Gary Turk (4:58): https://www.youtube.com/watch?v=Z7dLU6fk9QY#t=50
2. www.FilmsForAction.org (2:11): http://www.filmsforaction.org/watch /i_forgot_my_phone

13-6. A MAGAZINE IS AN IPAD THAT DOES NOT WORK

A one-year-old tries to make a magazine "work." Watch her fingers! (1:25)

http://www.youtube.com/watch?v=aXV-yaFmQNk

13-7. HANS ROSLING—TWO HUNDRED COUNTRIES, TWO HUNDRED YEARS

This video is a fascinating romp through two hundred years of the development of countries. Dr. Rosling (1948–2017) uses captivating graphics and animations to present statistics on how countries have developed. He was a world-renowned Swedish statistician who pointed out that the average number of legs in Swedish adults is 1.999, so most Swedes are above average. (4:47)

http://www.youtube.com/watch?v=jbkSRLYSojo

13-8. SIR HAROLD EVANS—WHO REALLY INVENTED THE FRANCHISE?

Martha Matilda Harper is not yet a household name. This Canadian-born maid started her business journey in 1888. Her story of creating franchises demonstrates what someone can accomplish with a new idea, little money, and a lot of determination. It is commonly thought that Ray Kroc, the founder of McDonald's, created franchising. Another TED video. (5:49)

http://ed.ted.com/lessons/the-real-origin-of-the-franchise

13-9. MONTY PYTHON—"THE ARGUMENT CLINIC"

One of the best Monty Python skits ever! (3:06)

https://www.youtube.com/watch?v=ohDB5gbtaEQ

14

Venturing Out

"Twenty years from now you will be more disappointed by the things you didn't do than by the ones you did do."

—Mark Twain (1835–1910)

14-1. HOW DO YOU PROCEED FROM HERE?

How do you proceed from here? Simple: choose a few ideas that you are comfortable with and run with them.

There is no secret to life! There are no secrets to learn, just knowledge to acquire. We all start with zero knowledge, then we make choices that enhance or detract from our daily lives. We discover things that work and don't work and learn accordingly. Hopefully, we learn from failures to make choices that lead to happier lives.

As you venture out into the real world, here are a few perspectives to take with you.

"Be kind, for everyone you meet is fighting a hard battle."

—Ian Maclaren (1850–1907)

On the futility of worrying:

"I've seen lots of trouble in my day, most of which never happened."

—*Mark Twain (1835–1910)*

On intellectual honesty:

"This above all: to thine own self be true,
and it must follow, as the night the day,
thou canst not then be false to any man."

—*William Shakespeare (1564–1616), in* Hamlet, *act 1, scene 3*

"Be who you are and say what you feel,
because those who mind don't matter,
and those who matter don't mind."

—*Theodor Geisel, aka Dr. Seuss (1904–1991)*

On life:

"Life is short, break the rules.
Forgive quickly, kiss SLOWLY.
Love truly. Laugh uncontrollably and never regret ANYTHING that makes you smile."

—*Mark Twain (1835–1910)*

Lastly, a definition of success adapted from a poem by Bessie A. Stanley (1879–1952):

To laugh often and much;
to win the respect of intelligent people and the affection of children;
to earn the appreciation of honest critics and endure the betrayal of false friends;
to appreciate beauty, to find the best in others;
to leave the world a bit better, whether by a healthy child, a garden patch or a redeemed social condition;
to know that even one life has breathed easier because YOU have lived.
This is to have succeeded.

Best of success to you!

References

One way to check out the references is to check them out of your local public library. You can reserve books and electronic media online, then pick them up when you receive notice that they are available. There is no additional charge to use the public library, and you save potentially thousands of dollars in expenses for books. (Note: References are listed alphabetically within each category.)

BOOKS AND MAGAZINES

Edwin A. Abbott, *Flatland*. A penetrating satire on society published in 1884 and still relevant today.

David Allen, *Getting Things Done*. A system for organizing tasks and projects.

Harry Beckwith, *Selling the Invisible*. Scores of tips on running a service business.

Ambrose Bierce, *The Devil's Dictionary*. A delightful satire on society based on defining words from a satirist's point of view.

George S. Clason, *The Richest Man in Babylon*. How to start building wealth and get out of debt, all told in parables about ancient Babylon.

Dr. Carol S. Dweck, *Mindset: The New Psychology of Success.* Explores growth vs. fixed mind-set and its effect on happiness and success.

Milo O. Frank, *How to Get Your Point Across in 30 Seconds or Less.* A short book. ☺

Hannah Fry, *Hello World: Being Human in the Age of Algorithms.* The subtitle says it all. Professor Fry explains succinctly how computers and algorithms are impacting society.

Daniel Goleman, *Emotional Intelligence: Why It Can Matter More Than IQ.* Explains the concepts behind Emotional Intelligence and how to improve yours.

Henry Hazlitt, *Economics in One Lesson.* Economics in one lesson.

Napoleon Hill, *Outwitting the Devil.* Challenges you to be intellectually honest and proactive, and explains how not to be a drifter in life. Don't read it if you're not willing to examine your beliefs.

Kay Redfield Jamison, *An Unquiet Mind.* Her own story about life with bipolar disorder.

Elisabeth Kübler-Ross, *On Death and Dying.* Dealing with the loss of a loved one.

Mad magazine. A delightful satire on society based on madcap humor.

William J. O'Neil, *How to Make Money in Stocks.* How to make money in stocks. www.investors.com. (Related: Matthew Galgani, *How to Make Money in Stocks: Getting Started*; Amy Smith, *How to Make Money in Stocks: Success Stories*)

Suze Orman, *The Money Book for the Young, Fabulous and Broke.* Orman has also written many other excellent books on financial matters.

Oxford English Dictionary (OED). The source for most definitions used in this book.

Tom Peters and Robert Waterman Jr., *In Search of Excellence.* How companies establish a culture of excellence.

Dr. Hans Selye, *The Stress of Life*. The first book to discuss stress and the human mind.

Marsha Sinetar, *Do What You Love, the Money Will Follow*. What you do with passion often leads to increased income.

William Strunk Jr. and E. B. White, *The Elements of Style*. The classic on writing well.

Bronnie Ware, *The Top Five Regrets of the Dying: A Life Transformed by the Dearly Departing*. People's perspectives as they prepare to die.

William Zinnser, *On Writing Well*. Another classic on writing well.

POEMS

Edmund Vance Cooke, "How Did You Die?"

Rudyard Kipling, "If"

ONLINE RESOURCES

Resources for How You Know You Are Right and for Semantic Precision

Contact Cheryl Cerell, Marketing Director of the Free Enterprise Institute: http://www.fei-ajg.com

Resources for Mental Health

Chrissie Hodges, *Pure OCD: The Invisible Side of Obsessive-Compulsive Disorder*

Kay Redfield Jamison, *An Unquiet Mind*. Her own story about life with bipolar disorder.

National Alliance on Mental Illness, www.nami.org. Resources, local support groups, and more.

National Institute of Mental Health, "What Is Bipolar Disorder?," http://www.nimh.nih.gov/health/topics/bipolar-disorder/index.shtml.

Other Sites

14ers.com. Great site for information on Fourteeners, Colorado's mountains with elevations over 14,000 feet. It has routes, trip reports from other climbers describing past and current conditions, facts, photos, and a lot more!

The following sites offer excellent material for self-esteem building, goal setting, success attainment, and business management. If you find a product you like, try locating it first at your public library to save some money.

NightingaleConant, http://www.nightingale.com/. Many resources for personal improvement.

TED, http://www.ted.com. Videos on a wide range of topics.

Brian Tracy, http://www.briantracy.com/. Motivational and sales speaker.

Dr. Denis Waitley, http://www.waitley.com/. High-performance human achievement.

Wordsmith, http://www.wordsmith.org. Boost vocabulary with a word of the day, Monday through Friday. No extra charge to become a subscriber.

Time Management and To-Do Lists

David Allen, *Getting Things Done.*

Evernote, www.evernote.com. Also available as a mobile app.

Kirby Alarm Pro, http://www.kirbyfooty.com/product-kirbyalarm.php.

Humor

George Carlin, a *clean* speech at the National Press Club, May 13, 1999, http://www.youtube.com/watch?v=Pc0ZHsoHAlE. On the funny yet intricate use of language. (56:30)

Inspiration

BrainyQuote, http://www.brainyquote.com/. Quotations from thousands of sources. (Or simply search for "inspirational quotes" and the name of a favorite person.)

StumbleUpon, http://www.StumbleUpon.com. "Pandora for the mind." Learns your preferences for different subjects and ideas, and presents you with new related material on the web.

About the Author

"When I'm perfect, I'll criticize" is an expression **David Kramer** coined out of respect for people with stories to tell about their own life journeys. (That's everyone!) Software-business entrepreneur turned university educator, David wants to help the next generation take its place in the world.

Born in 1949 in Brooklyn, New York—America!—David chose a career in 1961, at age twelve, in the newly emerging computer industry. Founder of two successful custom software companies, he started his teaching career, in 2000, at age fifty-one. To succeed personally and professionally, David uses two key approaches to life. The main one is accepting the love and support of family and friends. A close second is defining for himself such important aspirations as love, success, wealth, and other common terms often haphazardly thrown about and imposed on others.

David has two daughters, seven grandchildren, a BS in mathematics (Phi Beta Kappa), and an MS in computer science (with three excellence awards). He lives in Denver, Colorado, and enjoys anything having to do with Colorado's mountains, including climbing all fifty-four of its peaks above 14,000 feet.